Dear Reader,

Stressful situations abound in our lives. Tornadoes, flash floods, and hurricanes upend lives across the country. News of large-scale economic woes and terrorist attacks seems to play in endless loops. Day-to-day hassles may feel remarkably stressful, too. Traffic jams snarl your commute. Unpaid bills thunk into your virtual or actual mailbox. Work or family worries loom large. And while your to-do list grows exponentially, your free time may be in woefully short supply.

All of us have the same physiological response to stress: a rush of natural chemicals in the body instantly amplifies our strength and senses to help us take action. This swift reflex was encoded for our survival. Thanks to the stress response, you might jump out of the way of a speeding car or rush away from a burning building.

Yet abundant research shows us that too much stress can be harmful. When the stress response is repeatedly evoked for real and perceived threats—if you're running late to a meeting, let's say, or worrying about problems that may never occur—the chronic effects cause unnecessary wear and tear on your body, eroding your mental and physical health. Many well-respected studies link chronic stress to heart disease and stroke, the No. 1 and No. 4 causes of death in the United States. Stress is also implicated in a host of other ailments, including depression and anxiety, chronic lower respiratory diseases, high blood pressure, asthma flare-ups, and diabetes.

Fortunately, this strong connection between mind and body can work in your favor, too. Exciting new scientific breakthroughs show—right down to the level of genes and molecules—how stress management can benefit your body. This report will help you learn techniques for managing stress, enabling you to lower your risks for developing certain health problems and to keep some ailments from worsening. A major way of doing this is by eliciting the relaxation response, using two simple steps to put your body in a calm, relaxed state—the very opposite of the stress response. Together with other stress management techniques, these tools help build resiliency.

Often, we can't change the world around us. What we can change is how we perceive stressful situations and how resilient we are when faced with the minor and major troubles that arise in our lives, day by day, week by week. So, please, turn the pages of this special report. Find out how stress affects you, and learn how managing it through a variety of proven approaches can help you enhance your health and happiness.

Sincerely,

Herbert Benson, M.D.
Medical Editor

Aggie Casey, M.S., R.N.
Medical Editor

Understanding the stress response

Stress is an unavoidable part of life. But learning to manage it successfully can do much to improve your mental and physical health. In later sections, we'll highlight some exciting new research that shows, on the level of your genes, just why stress management is such a powerful tool. We'll give you a smorgasbord of techniques for coping with stressful situations, too.

But first, it helps to understand just how your body reacts to stressful situations—and why the so-called fight-or-flight response, which can be lifesaving in the case of an immediate physical threat, becomes detrimental when stress is a chronic feature of daily life.

What is stress?

We all encounter stress in our lives, though we might use different examples to describe it. You might define stress as bumper-to-bumper traffic, a deadline bearing down fast, a worrisome illness, or a contentious argument with your partner. A friend may define it as a relationship spiraling downward, the need to care for an ailing parent, or an email chime heralding yet another unpaid bill.

If you were a medical expert, though, you would label these stressors—that is, examples of stressful events and circumstances. And you would define stress more specifically as an automatic physical response to such challenges, or indeed to any situation that requires you to adapt to change.

Whether the particular stressor you're confronting is a sudden car crash, a loud argument, or the ache of arthritis, each potential or actual threat triggers a cascade of stress hormones that produce well-orchestrated physiological changes.

You know these sensations well. Your heart pounds. Muscles tense. Breathing quickens, and beads of sweat appear. But exactly how and why these reactions occur and what effects they might have when repeatedly evoked over time are questions that have intrigued researchers for years.

Harvard physiologist Walter B. Cannon was a pioneer in exploring the biochemistry of stress. Nearly a century ago, his research convinced him that fright was not all in the mind, but also involved a physical response. By experimenting with barking dogs and caged cats, Cannon was able to isolate a hormone secreted by the adrenal glands of cats when they were frightened. When he injected that hormone into a second, perfectly calm cat, it touched off a physical reaction of fear. The cat's heartbeat and blood pressure shot up, while blood flow to the muscles increased. Cannon dubbed this occurrence the "fright, fight, or flight" response. Today we know it as the fight-or-flight response, or the stress response.

A look inside the stress response

Cannon's discovery was correct, as far as it went. But since then, scientists have learned a great deal more about the body's reaction to stress. It involves not just one hormone, but a series of hormones, the brain, and a part of the nervous system called the autonomic nervous system, which rules involuntary body functions such as breathing, blood pressure, and heartbeat.

Our response to threats begins in the brain, which receives and processes information—perhaps the sight of your boss bearing down with an ominous expression, or the sound of an explosion. Instantly, a signal from the motor cortex in the brain speeds down nerve pathways to muscles, which tense and tighten, bracing for trouble. Another signal comes from the hypothalamus, a portion of the brain perched above the brainstem. It relays the warning to the nearby pituitary gland, which sends a chemical messenger via the bloodstream to the adrenal glands. In response, the adrenal glands secrete a series of stress hormones, including the first hormone that Cannon isolated—epinephrine, better known as adrenaline. You're probably familiar with the so-called adrenaline rush that helps rev up your body. This is part of the stress response.

The adrenal glands also release a second stress hormone identified by Cannon, called norepinephrine, or noradrenaline. Other researchers added a third discovery—the stress hormone cortisol. When you're faced with a stressful situation, all three begin coursing through your bloodstream, producing a broad range of physiological responses (see Figure 1, page 4).

Simultaneously, the hypothalamus fires up the autonomic nervous system. This network of nerves relays the warning down through the spinal cord and from there to nerves throughout the body. In response, nerve endings in organs, blood vessels, the skin, and even sweat glands release epinephrine and norepinephrine.

This tandem surge of hormones primes your body to react to the imminent threat. In the case of an immediate physical danger, such as the sudden appearance of a prowling wild animal or an armed enemy, you respond by either preparing to stand your ground and fight, or else fleeing to safety. Either way, you need to gear up for action, which is precisely what stress hormones enable you to do.

Your breath quickens as your body takes in extra oxygen to help fuel your muscles. Likewise, energy-boosting glucose and fats are released from storage sites into your bloodstream. Sharpened senses, such as sight and hearing, make you more alert.

Your heart pounds—beating up to two to three times as quickly as normal—and your blood pressure rises. Certain blood vessels constrict, which helps direct blood flow to your muscles and brain and away from your skin and other organs.

Blood cells called platelets become stickier, so clots can form more easily to minimize bleeding from potential injuries. Immune system activity picks up. Your muscles—even tiny, hair-raising muscles beneath your skin—tighten, preparing you to spring into action.

Body systems not needed for the immediate emergency are suppressed in order to focus energy where it's needed. The stomach and intestines cease operations. Sexual arousal lessens. Repair and growth of body tissues slows.

> **Try this now**

Feeling stressed? A few quick body checks can answer that question:

- ✔ Are you breathing shallowly? Put one hand on your chest and the other on your belly. When you breathe in and out, pay attention to which hand is moving. Calming breaths draw air deep into your lungs, so that your chest and belly expand; shallow, tense breaths involve only your chest.
- ✔ Are your neck and shoulders tense? Take a deep breath. As you breathe out, slowly roll your shoulders up toward your ears, back, and down, relaxing them as much as possible. Are your shoulders lower than they were a moment ago?
- ✔ Are you clenching your jaw or your fists? Take a deep breath, then relax your jaw until your lips are slightly parted. Take another deep breath and relax your hands so that your fingers are loosely parted.

For a more complete list of stress warning signs, see "My stress warning signs," page 22. Then, for a series of exercises to help drain tension, try the relaxation response techniques starting on page 24. You'll be surprised at how thoroughly relaxed your body can feel.

Defusing the stress response

Cannon believed the stress response was temporary. Minutes after the rush triggered by epinephrine, he thought, a peron's body would wind down to its normal state of balance, known as homeostasis. The lungs would slow their rate of breathing. Blood pressure would drop as the heartbeat slowed and blood flowed in normal patterns again. The intestines would resume their work, providing new fuel to replace the energy burned in the emergency. Bone and skin cells would resume repairs or grow again, as needed. Sex might appear more inviting.

Later research showed, however, that Cannon was not completely correct. Often, the effects of stress linger for an extended period of time, or may even compound so that the body never completely unwinds.

The autonomic nervous system, it turns out, is divided into two parts with opposite effects. The sympathetic nervous system revs up the body in response to perceived dangers, as described above. Its counterpart, the parasympathetic nervous system, calms the body after the danger has passed. But in today's society, stressors often pile up one after another in a combination of traffic jams, deadlines, money woes, and a host of other challenges that fill our days rather than passing rapidly, like the wild animal that eventually lumbers away. As a result, the sympathetic system often remains engaged long after it should have yielded to the soothing influence of the parasympathetic system. The results can be damaging in many ways (see "The importance of stress reduction," page 6).

Even faced with chronic stress, however, you can benefit from stress management techniques. Regular use of these techniques can help you tamp down the sympathetic nervous system when it is not truly needed and restore balance (see "Managing your stress through the relaxation response," page 24).

The positive effects of short-term stress

As many people have noted, the stress response can be enormously helpful in times of physical danger. Surging epinephrine (adrenaline) enables people to perform Herculean feats. Abundant proof of this is offered by the first responders, firefighters, and ordinary citizens who acted swiftly to help others as Hurricane Sandy raged up the East Coast, bombs exploded at the Boston Marathon, or tornadoes and wildfires devastated parts of the Midwest and the West.

The stress response is appropriate and essential in such overwhelming situations. When appropriately evoked, the stress response helps us rise to many challenges. These challenges may be external forces, such as a fire or an earthquake, or internal threats, such as your circulatory system teetering on the brink of a deadly collapse.

Over the years, many intriguing questions about stress have been asked and answered. A physiologist named Hans Selye, whose work helped shape modern stress theory, advanced the idea that psychosocial stressors like a pressing work deadline or a heated family argument trigger the same physiological response as a physical threat. Selye explored the link between short-term stress that stimulates people to summon the resources to hurdle obstacles ("good" stress) and ongoing or overabundant stress, which wears down our ability to adapt and cope ("bad" stress, or distress).

Two Harvard researchers, Robert M. Yerkes and John D. Dodson, likewise demonstrated that a jolt of stress isn't necessarily bad. It can help with non-Herculean tasks like finishing a difficult project or juggling a tight schedule. They noted that as stress or anxiety levels rose, so did performance and efficiency—up to

Figure 1: The stress response

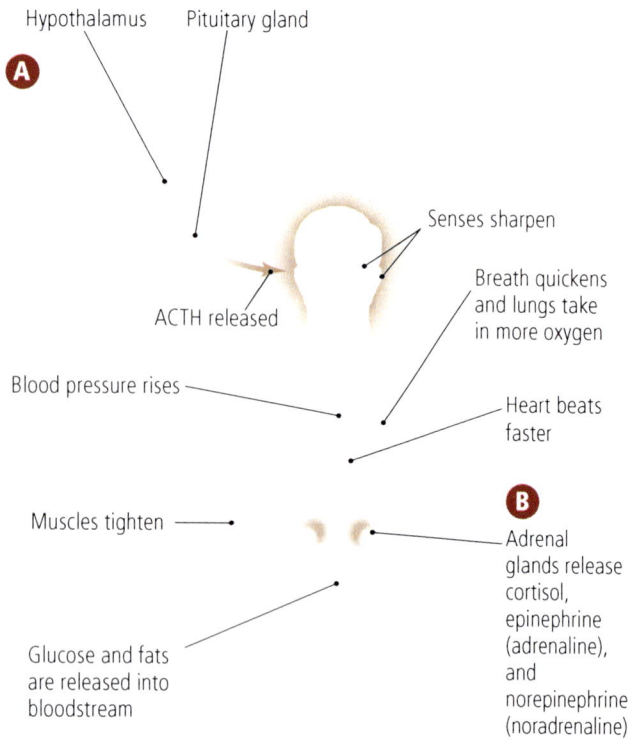

Collectively, the hypothalamus, pituitary gland, and adrenal glands make up the HPA axis, which plays a pivotal role in triggering the stress response. The hypothalamus sends a chemical messenger (corticotropin-releasing factor, or CRF) to the nearby pituitary gland, which then releases its own chemical messenger (adrenocorticotropic hormone, or ACTH) into the bloodstream **(A)**. ACTH travels to the adrenal glands, which respond by releasing a number of stress hormones into the bloodstream **(B)**.

At the same time, the sympathetic nervous system releases stress hormones, too (not shown). The combined effects of these hormones are widespread, as this illustration reveals. Senses become sharper, muscles tighten, the heart beats faster, blood pressure rises, and breathing quickens. All of this prepares you to fight or flee in the face of danger.

a point (see Figure 2, below). Once this optimal point was reached, however, further stress and anxiety led to significant declines in performance and ability.

Where the turning point falls seems to differ from person to person, for while the stress response is hardwired into humans and other animals, the events and perceptions that set it off vary widely. What you perceive as a threatening situation, your neighbor may easily brush aside or even relish.

Scientists have tackled the question of why some people appear less vulnerable to stress or even seem to thrive on it. Research has identified characteristics common to stress-hardy folks. Exercise and social support proved essential. So did control, challenge, and commitment. Stress-hardy people seem to feel a sense of control or the ability to influence events. They embrace the challenge in situations others might find stressful and describe themselves as committed to something meaningful. Research shows that people with these characteristics report fewer illnesses and are less likely to be absent from work.

The negative effects of chronic stress

Intuitively, the stress response makes sense. It enables us to rise to occasions and events that reward heightened awareness and abilities. You hear a tree limb crack above you while sheltering from a storm, and the surge of epinephrine helps you sprint out of its path far faster than you normally move. The stress hormones that spilled into your bloodstream found the perfect physical outlet.

But experience tells us obvious dangers are not the only scenarios that elicit the stress response. Any situation you perceive as a hassle or threat to your well-being may trigger it, too, especially if a lightning-quick assessment suggests that you don't have the resources to cope with it. And that's where trouble starts.

Your body does a poor job of distinguishing between life-threatening events and day-to-day stressful situations. Anger or anxiety triggered by less momentous sources of stress, such as computer meltdowns or traffic jams, doesn't find a quick physical release and tends to build up as the day rolls on. Adding to the turmoil is anticipation of potential problems when, say, layoff rumors fly or medical test results are delayed. Without realizing it, you might make assumptions about whether you'll be laid off or what the test results will show, setting off another cycle of physiological symptoms—such as a clenched jaw, tight neck and shoulders, and anxiety.

When your body repeatedly experiences the stress response, or when arousal following a terrible trauma is never fully switched off (see "Post-traumatic stress disorder," page 8), your body's stress response can be described as maladaptive, or unhealthy. In this situation, the stress response kicks in sooner or more frequently than normal, increasing the burden your body must handle. Maladaptive stress responses can lead to worrisome health problems. A prime example of this is high blood pressure, or hypertension, which is a major risk factor for coronary artery disease. Another is suppression of the immune system, which increases susceptibility to colds and other common illnesses (see "The importance of stress reduction," page 6).

It's impossible to sidestep all sources of stress. Would you really want to, anyway? Our lives are full of physical and psychological challenges that add zest to life and sometimes deliver satisfying rewards. But while you can't easily erase all sources of stress, you can learn to perceive and handle them differently. You'll learn how in "Managing your stress through the relaxation response" (see page 24) and "Expanding your toolbox for managing stress" (see page 33).

Figure 2: The ups and downs of stress

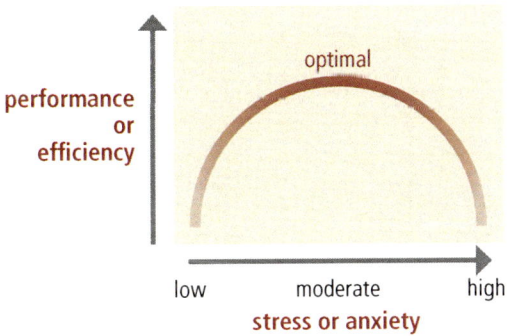

Researchers Robert M. Yerkes and John D. Dodson showed that as stress increases, performance rises to an optimal point, but if stress continues to increase, eventually performance and efficiency decline. This is known as the Yerkes-Dodson law.

The importance of stress reduction

Skeptics have long believed that meditation and other stress reduction techniques are nice but ineffectual practices that do little for you. Nothing could be further from the truth—and now we have the science to prove it.

There is no doubt that chronic stress has negative effects on the body, and it acts in multiple ways. To begin with, the ripple effects of stress undermine healthy behavior. If you've ever powered your way through a taxing day on a fistful of candy bars and cigarettes, you understand the issue firsthand. But over and above such impacts on behavior, stress has direct effects on the body.

Abundant evidence shows that chronic stress chips away at physical health, pushing blood pressure to dizzying heights and harming the heart. It plays a role in diabetes, asthma, and gastrointestinal disorders. Stress suppresses the immune system and may hamper recovery from illnesses ranging from the common cold to cancer. Emerging research also supports the notion that high levels of stress may even speed up the aging process.

By contrast, people exhibiting less stress tend to be in better health, and now we're starting to understand why. Intriguing new science suggests that regularly eliciting the relaxation response—a natural counterbalance to the stress response—can act on our genes in ways that may evoke multiple health benefits and help reduce the harmful effects of stress (see "Genes and the relaxation response," next). Small studies of various stress reduction techniques, as well as comprehensive programs like the one described in this report, suggest that it's quite possible to improve many measures of health by making the strong mind-body connection work in your favor.

Keep in mind, though, that while stress management techniques can help in multiple ways, serious health conditions require medical treatment, too. Your doctor can recommend the treatment plan that's best for you.

Genes and the relaxation response

Exciting new research from the Benson-Henry Institute for Mind Body Medicine at Massachusetts General Hospital suggests that the simple act of eliciting the relaxation response (and thereby dialing back the stress response) temporarily changes the activity of certain genes in ways that may benefit health. For starters, it switches off genes associated with chronic inflammatory responses. Many experts believe these inflammatory responses stress the body, possibly contributing to a host of chronic ailments, such as heart disease, inflammatory bowel disease, and diabetes. At the same time, it switches on genes linked with a variety of functions: the use of energy in the body, the release of insulin (which helps regulate blood sugar), the maintenance of telomeres (protective endcaps on our chromosomes that erode with age until a cell dies), and the functions of tiny cellular powerhouses called mitochondria. The researchers speculate that the latter may create energy reserves that help the body counter oxidative stress that can harm cells.

For this study, the researchers recruited two small groups of healthy subjects: long-term practitioners of techniques like yoga, meditation, and repetitive prayer that elicit the relaxation response; and novices who hadn't used these techniques. The novices were tested

> "People have been using a variety of relaxation response techniques for many years—think of yoga, for example. Now we've uncovered a scientific framework that supports some of the beneficial effects."
>
> —Dr. Herbert Benson, director emeritus of the Benson-Henry Institute for Mind Body Medicine

initially after listening to a health education tape—this allowed them to serve as a control group. They then learned a sequence of relaxation response techniques, which they practiced for 20 minutes a day, guided by a CD, over eight weeks. This sequence included diaphragmatic breathing (also known as breath focus), body scan, mantra repetition, and mindfulness meditation (see "Managing your stress through the relaxation response," page 24).

To gauge the changes in gene activity, the researchers obtained blood samples from the groups immediately before a single relaxation response session, immediately afterward, and 15 minutes afterward. While the long-term practitioners had the most profound changes in gene activity, the group with eight weeks of training also experienced significant changes in gene activity compared with results they'd posted as complete novices.

These results built on the findings of an earlier study conducted by the Genomics Center at Beth Israel Deaconness Medical Center and the Benson-Henry Institute for Mind Body Medicine that found similar results, with changes in the activity of genes controlling how the body handles free radicals, inflammatory processes, and cell death. Once again, greater changes were seen in the long-term practitioners than in the novices.

Aiming for lasting benefits

Gene activity isn't altered forever by yoga or repetitive prayer. One lesson gleaned from these studies is that the relaxation response must be regularly elicited in order to make beneficial changes persist. Additional research needs to be done to learn whether similar changes occur in people who use relaxation response techniques to help treat stress-related illnesses. Already, studies examining the effects of relaxation techniques on hypertension, inflammatory bowel syndrome, and multiple myeloma are under way.

Health problems that are linked to stress

Stress may contribute to or exacerbate health problems from A to Z (or at least to U). Among them:

- allergic skin reactions
- anxiety
- arthritis
- constipation
- cough
- depression
- diabetes
- dizziness
- gum disease
- headaches
- heart problems, such as angina (chest pains), arrhythmias, heart attack, and palpitations (pounding heart)
- heartburn
- high blood pressure
- infectious diseases, such as colds or herpes
- infertility
- insomnia and resulting fatigue
- irritable bowel syndrome
- menopausal symptoms, such as hot flashes
- "morning sickness," the nausea and vomiting of pregnancy
- nervousness
- pain of any sort, including backaches, headaches, abdominal pain, muscle pain, joint aches, postoperative pain, and chronic pain caused by many conditions
- Parkinson's disease
- postoperative swelling
- premenstrual syndrome (PMS)
- side effects of AIDS
- side effects of cancer and cancer treatments
- slow wound healing
- ulcers.

To the extent that stress worsens these ailments, the relaxation response (a state of profound rest) and other stress management methods can be healing. More in-depth information about some of the medical effects of stress and the benefits of stress management can be found throughout this section.

Adapted from The Relaxation Revolution, Herbert Benson, M.D., and William Proctor, J.D. (Scribner, 2010).

Post-traumatic stress disorder (PTSD)

Imagine this: You're a soldier on leave walking down a city street with your family. You notice an ominous grouping of trash cans out of the corner of your eye, or maybe a truck driving toward you backfires loudly. Before you know it, you've launched yourself at your children, knocking them to the ground to take cover from the explosion. Like a rubber band, the sights and sounds snapped you back to your trained response to IEDs—improvised explosive devices—in a combat zone.

Traumatic experiences often scar the psyche. Many military personnel who have been in combat suffer post-traumatic stress disorder (PTSD). According to the National Center for Posttraumatic Stress Disorder, 14% of veterans of the Iraq and Afghanistan wars, 10% of Gulf War veterans, and as many as 30% of Vietnam veterans have experienced PTSD.

Other traumatic events—such as rape, physical assault, accidents, natural disasters, witnessing acts of terrorism, living in a war zone or otherwise violent locale, losing a loved one suddenly, or even having a heart attack—may also trigger PTSD. A national survey estimated that nearly 4% of men and 10% of women will experience PTSD during their lifetimes. The risk is higher among people with a family history of depression.

Key symptoms of PTSD are

- recurrent flashbacks, dreams, or intrusive thoughts about a traumatic event
- withdrawal from people and certain situations
- avoidance of reminders of the event or difficulty recalling it
- difficulty sleeping
- being overly vigilant or easily startled.

Not everyone who survives a traumatic event develops PTSD. Even if your immediate response to a disaster is extreme, this is not a sign of an emotional disorder or mental illness. Reaching out to others and resuming normal life may provide solace. Physical activity and expressing emotions while concentrating on the future may also prove useful. Eliciting the relaxation response regularly, or using other stress management tools, can help, too. Our "blue dot" exercise, a visual reminder to engage in frequent mini-relaxations when faced with situations likely to set off a stress reaction, may help keep you on a calmer track (see "Blue dots," page 28).

If PTSD symptoms disrupt your life or affect you for more than a few weeks, seek help from a licensed mental health professional. Keep in mind, too, that sometimes symptoms don't occur until six months or more after the triggering event.

Cardiovascular disease

Cardiovascular disease encompasses a range of ailments that affect the heart or impinge upon the thousands of miles of blood vessels that nurture cells throughout the body. Three obvious examples are atherosclerosis (the accumulation of fatty deposits on artery walls), heart attacks, and high blood pressure (see page 10). Chronic stress contributes to all three. Stress can also trigger atrial fibrillation, palpitations, premature ventricular contractions, and other arrhythmias (abnormal heart rhythms).

The landmark Framingham Heart Study noted that a number of risk factors for cardiovascular disease are beyond your control (race, age, gender, and genetics). However, you can control other risk factors such as smoking, inactivity, obesity, high blood cholesterol, and type 2 diabetes—and, of course, stress. A variety of psychological and social factors with stress-related dimensions—including depression, anxiety, anger and hostility, a lack of social support, work stress, marital stress, low socioeconomic status, and caregiver strain—also play significant roles in the development of cardiovascular disease. Acting alone, each of these factors heightens the chances of developing heart trouble. When combined, their power increases exponentially.

One three-year study asked 2,700 American adults to complete an online survey of physical and mental health following the terrorist attacks of Sept. 11, 2001. People who had high levels of stress immediately after the attacks were nearly twice as likely to develop high blood pressure and more than three times as likely to develop other heart problems during the following two years compared with those who had low stress levels.

Even our perceptions about how stress affects us may be harmful, according to a study tracking 7,200 British men and women, which was published in the *European Heart Journal* in 2013. People who believed stress had affected their health "a lot or extremely" were twice as likely to die from heart disease or have a nonfatal heart attack, compared with those who reported stress was not harming them.

How exactly might stress contribute to cardiovascular disease? Several avenues are under study. The release of stress hormones, such as epinephrine, into the bloodstream appears to increase the amount of cholesterol made by the body. In addition, when the sympathetic nervous system is aroused, blood pressure rises and platelets become stickier (see "A look inside the stress response," page 2). Stickier platelets make blood clots more likely, while ongoing high blood pressure damages the heart, blood vessels, and other organs, and greatly increases your chances of developing heart disease, if the stress response is being repeatedly evoked.

Chronic inflammation—known to play a key role in the development of heart disease, and apparently exacerbated by chronic stress—is another possible player here. In times of need, inflammation serves many useful functions. It defends the body against bacteria, viruses, and other foreign invaders, removes debris, and helps repair damaged tissue. Inside arteries, however, chronic low-grade inflammation contributes to the development of atherosclerosis. Atherosclerosis in turn can narrow blood vessels dangerously, causing chest pain, a heart attack, or a stroke (see Figure 3, at right). Chronic inflammation even influences the formation of artery-blocking clots, the ultimate cause of heart attacks and many strokes.

Stress has indirect influences, too, when negative emotions shape behaviors that affect cardiovascular risk. For example, people who are stressed are more likely to smoke and less likely to be physically active.

In some vulnerable people, research also shows that sudden spasms in coronary arteries can be brought on by mental stress—at least when people with existing heart disease are asked to do complex equations during laboratory experiments. A sudden spasm can block blood flow to part of the heart, causing chest pain or even a heart attack.

An ambitious research project published in *The Lancet*, which involved over 24,000 participants from 52 countries, demonstrated the role of stress in heightening heart attack risk. Roughly 11,000 people who had just had a first heart attack were asked, as they left the hospital, about various forms of stress they had experienced in the preceding 12 months. The questions probed reactions to job and home stress, financial problems, and major life events. Members of a control group, who were matched to the heart attack patients for age and gender but who had no history of heart disease, underwent similar assessments. Despite variations in the prevalence of stress across countries and ethnic groups, increased stress levels conferred a greater risk for heart attack than did hypertension, abdominal obesity, diabetes, and several other risk factors.

Can stress management help?

Yes. The strongest evidence for the benefits of stress management springs from heart disease studies. Certainly, it appears that treating depression, controlling anger and hostility, and improving social support could lower your odds of developing heart disease.

Figure 3: Inside a narrowed artery

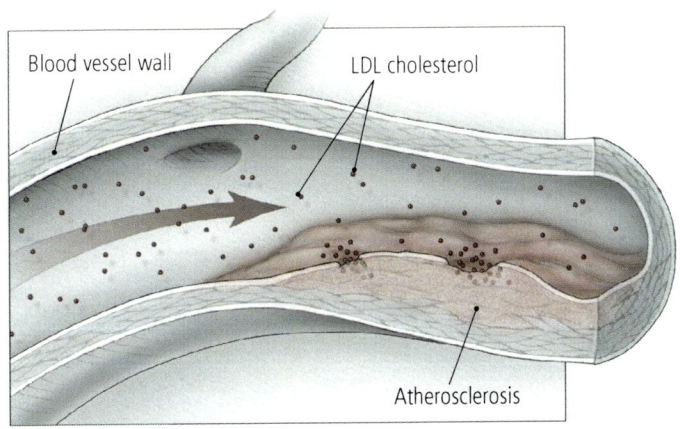

Stress may damage your arteries in several ways. Chronic stress can lead to high blood pressure, which causes tiny tears and scarring in artery walls that trap plaque. Some research suggests stress may boost inflammatory markers that harm blood vessels, too. Scientists also theorize that stress hormones increase cholesterol levels. People with high levels of low-density lipoprotein (LDL) cholesterol are more likely to develop atherosclerosis, which is the buildup of fatty deposits on artery walls. As the mixture of fats, calcium deposits, and cell debris accumulates on artery walls, the channel that the blood flows through becomes progressively narrower. Eventually, blood flow is obstructed. The blockage can cause angina, a heart attack, or stroke.

The impact of stress on diabetes

Nearly 26 million Americans are estimated to have diabetes. Some know it; some don't. The vast majority—90% to 95%—have type 2 diabetes, which is often triggered by obesity, poor diet, and inactivity. Another 79 million Americans are skating close to that edge with higher-than-normal blood glucose (sugar) levels, a condition called prediabetes.

While chronic stress isn't thought to cause diabetes, it can make blood sugar harder to control, a problem that compounds if you're using unhealthy behaviors to relieve pressure (see "Healthy vs. unhealthy responses to stress," page 22). Keeping blood sugar levels within certain parameters set by your doctor can help you prevent, or slow down, the many complications that stem from diabetes. Heart disease (the No. 1 cause of death in people with diabetes), nephropathy (kidney damage or disease), and psychosocial distress (depression, negative outlook, and similar issues) are among them.

The Heidelberger Diabetes and Stress Study (HEIDIS) is a five-year randomized, controlled trial of 110 people with type 2 diabetes. Half the group is serving as controls, while the other half engaged in an eight-week mindfulness-based stress reduction program that included meditation and a component aimed at handling difficult thoughts and feelings about diabetes. After six months, the mindfulness participants took part in a booster session. Thus far, first-year results show no effect on a key biomarker of nephropathy, but the mindfulness group had lower diastolic blood pressure and less distress and depression than the controls.

It's too soon to say whether a broad program of stress management can help people with diabetes gain better control over blood sugar levels—this isn't a point of investigation for HEIDIS—but signs certainly point in that direction. We already know that nurturing yourself by getting sufficient exercise and eating well, as well as losing excess weight, do double duty by helping your heart and, possibly, by lessening your need for diabetes medication. And of course, lowering your blood pressure, as the relaxation response has been shown to do, will help your heart, too.

Moreover, a Medicare-sponsored study published in the *American Heart Journal* in 2013 offers evidence that comprehensive stress management programs can help if you already have heart disease. This long-term study of 589 people with heart disease examined one-year programs aimed at improving cardiovascular health through lifestyle modifications, including stress management, exercise, and nutrition counseling. Two nationally recognized programs were evaluated: the Cardiac Wellness Program of the Benson-Henry Institute for Mind Body Medicine and the Dr. Dean Ornish Program for Reversing Heart Disease.

Both programs had a positive effect on cardiac risk factors: people lost weight, reduced their blood pressure levels, improved cholesterol levels, and reported greater psychological well-being. Both programs also appeared to improve cardiac function. Moreover, participants in the Benson-Henry program (which was created by Aggie Casey and Dr. Herbert Benson, the medical editors of this report) also had lower death rates and were less likely to be hospitalized for heart problems, compared with controls. The study concluded that these kinds of intensive lifestyle modification programs are clinically effective. While this study is good news for those with heart disease, more studies are needed to confirm these results.

High blood pressure

High blood pressure (hypertension) is a type of cardiovascular disease for which stress management seems particularly effective. The pumping action of your heart keeps blood circulating throughout your body, carrying nutrients and oxygen to billions of cells and carting off carbon dioxide and other metabolic debris to the organs responsible for their disposal. The force that moves the blood along is measured as blood pressure. Blood pressure fluctuates throughout the day, spiking when you exercise or get upset and dipping when you rest quietly or sleep.

The release of stress hormones causes your heart to beat faster and your blood pressure to rise. Often, this increase is temporary, and your heartbeat slows and your blood pressure drops once a threat has passed. But if the stress response is triggered repeatedly, blood pressure may remain consistently high.

High blood pressure is dangerous for several reasons. It forces the heart to pump harder to circulate blood. Eventually, the muscles of the heart respond by thickening. But this doesn't necessarily translate into added strength. In fact, often the heart's blood supply doesn't increase to the same degree, and, over time, the heart weakens. This can lead to heart failure (formerly known as congestive heart failure).

High blood pressure also damages artery walls in a way that promotes atherosclerosis. By narrowing arteries and interfering with blood flow, atherosclerosis can lead to a host of health problems, including angina (chest pain), heart attack, stroke, vision problems or loss, and kidney damage (see Figure 4, below). In fact, the higher your blood pressure, the greater your risk for heart attack, heart failure, stroke, and kidney disease.

Can stress management help?

Yes. Eliciting the relaxation response helps lower blood pressure. That happens in the short term, when you simply breathe deeply for several minutes to calm your body down. Frequent practice of the relaxation response techniques described in this report could help you reap more lasting benefits.

Sometimes medication is necessary to reduce high blood pressure to healthy levels. A randomized, controlled trial of older adults showed that an eight-week program of relaxation response plus other stress management techniques lessened the amount of medication some people needed to take in order to control their blood pressure.

Gastrointestinal disorders

Over a decade ago, an influential paper published in the journal *Gut* reported that a combination of psychological and physical factors can trigger gastrointestinal pain and other bowel symptoms. Severe life stress, the report also noted, often precedes the onset of functional bowel disorders for people being treated in gastrointestinal clinics. Laboratory experiments show the digestive system responds to emotional arousal and mental stress. Gastric acid secretion can increase, which may lead to heartburn and inflammation of the esophagus. Stress may play a role in the development of ulcers, too (see "Stress and ulcers," page 12). Stress can also cause abnormal contractions

Figure 4: High blood pressure and kidney damage

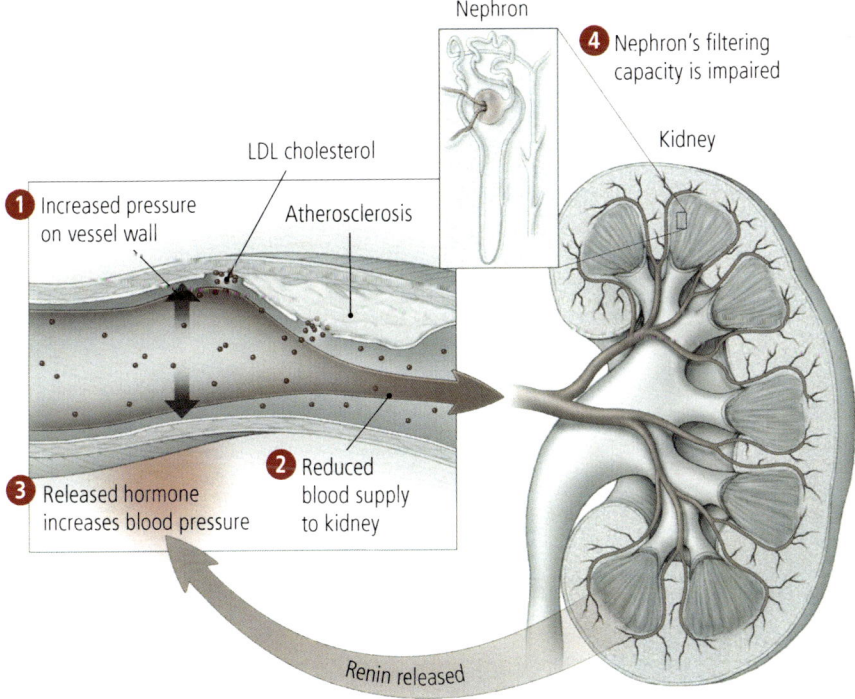

Stress can contribute to high blood pressure, setting the stage for atherosclerosis and sometimes kidney damage. High blood pressure causes tiny cracks in the lining of arteries. These cracks provide a breeding ground for fatty deposits. As the deposits accumulate along artery walls, blood flow is hampered. If the arteries that feed blood to the kidneys are affected, the body reacts by producing renin, a hormone that causes small arteries known as arterioles to narrow further. This kicks off a cycle of even higher blood pressure and further kidney damage. Over time, the diminished blood flow can damage or destroy the nephrons, the tiny filtering units inside your kidneys. When this happens, the kidney cannot filter wastes properly.

> ### Stress and ulcers
>
> People with ulcers used to be routinely advised to eat bland foods and cut sources of stress from their lives. Then scientists identified the bacterium *Helicobacter pylori* as a key instigator in the development of peptic ulcers, and antibiotics became the weapon of choice to combat them. Now the pendulum is swinging back, at least partway. A 13-year study of more than 4,000 people found that those who believed their lives were stressful were nearly twice as likely to get ulcers.
>
> Experts believe that stress may hamper the body's ability to repair the wall of the gut. Many studies have found that stress affects wound healing, which could have implications for ulcers, even those created by bacteria. One well-known experiment with medical students, for example, found that small incisions made in the forearm three days before a major exam took 40% longer to heal on average than when given during summer vacation.
>
> Stress might affect ulcers in other ways, too. It may trigger more gastric secretions, which increase inflammation and lessen the body's ability to buffer gastric acids.

in the small intestine and colon and affect the pace at which food travels through the gastrointestinal tract. Moreover, it affects the permeability of the intestines and regeneration of a layer of cells called the mucosa, which helps defend the body against harmful pathogens—and stress harms the beneficial bacteria that contribute to a healthy gut.

The parasympathetic nervous system, which brings the body back to normal after the stress response occurs (see "Defusing the stress response," page 3) is responsible for the change in colon contractions and the increase in gastric acid. Two English gastroenterologists found that when people with irritable bowel syndrome (IBS) who usually suffered from constipation were under stress, food moved more slowly through the small intestine. The opposite held true for those who typically had diarrhea.

A wide variety of triggers may cause IBS to flare up. Among them are a high-fat diet; alcoholic or caffeinated drinks and drinks that use a lot of artificial sweeteners; stress hormones that affect the gastrointestinal tract; and everyday stressors, such as arguments or work pressures. Some research suggests that the early loss of one or both parents through death or divorce results in higher-than-average rates of IBS and peptic ulcer disease.

Can stress management help?

Quite possibly, yes, if you suffer from IBS. A study that was published in the *American Journal of Gastroenterology* randomly assigned 75 women with IBS to eight weekly sessions plus an intensive half-day of mindfulness training, or to a support group. Immediately after treatment and at the three-month follow-up, mindfulness participants reported a much greater reduction in bowel symptoms than women in the support group. Measures of quality of life, psychological distress, and anxiety stemming from gastrointestinal sensations didn't change immediately for either group, yet were better at the three-month follow-up for the mindfulness participants. Not all studies agree that mindfulness training affects IBS symptoms, however.

Another promising stress management tool for people with IBS is cognitive behavioral therapy (CBT; see "Cognitive restructuring," page 33). One recent study compared the effects of 10 weeks of Internet-based CBT techniques guided by online therapists versus being on a waiting list. One aim of the therapy was to break the negative cycle linking avoidance behaviors, severity of symptoms, and impaired function (for example, avoiding work meetings or public transportation when feeling abdominal pain because of fear of losing bowel control). While treatment effects were small, CBT delivered via Internet was indeed effective for some people.

Along with IBS medications, dietary changes, exercise, and probiotics, the National Institute of Diabetes and Digestive and Kidney Diseases recommends trying stress management strategies, such as meditation and mindfulness, hypnotherapy, CBT, and other forms of psychotherapy. Talk to your doctor about tailoring a program that will best fit your situation.

Anxiety and depression

Stress feeds negative emotions like anxiety and depression. And, in turn, anxiety and depression may boost feelings of stress. Broadly speaking, depression may be sparked by thoughts of loss—a job layoff, a divorce, or a death, for example—and anxiety is typically tied to fear of the unknown.

Even when a clear threat to your well-being forms the springboard, anxious or depressive thoughts often spiral into a series of perceived threats, spinning off into increasingly distorted worries. A cancer diagnosis morphs instantly into a death sentence. The traffic jam that caused you to miss a meeting becomes an iron-clad reason for your boss to fire you.

If your anxiety is severe enough to interfere with daily life, talk to your doctor or seek counseling on your own. Symptoms may include any of the following:
- extreme worry or fear much of the time, or repeated panicky feelings
- irrational feelings of fear, dread, or danger
- frequent physical symptoms—such as agitation, shakiness and trembling, nausea, hot and cold flashes, dizziness, shortness of breath, or frequent urination—in the absence of a rational threat
- recurring distressing thoughts and uncontrollable repetitive behaviors intended to reduce the anxiety triggered by those thoughts.

Likewise, it's important to seek help from your doctor or a mental health professional if you have the following symptoms of depression:
- prolonged feelings of sadness or irritability
- loss of interest in activities you once enjoyed
- sleeping or eating markedly more or less than usual
- feelings of guilt, worthlessness, or hopelessness
- feeling anxious and unable to sit still
- trouble concentrating and making decisions.

Recurring thoughts of death or suicide are symptoms of depression that call for immediate professional attention.

Can stress management help?

Maybe. According to the National Center for Complementary and Alternative Medicine, relaxation response techniques can reduce anxiety prompted by stressful situations and may help address phobias or panic disorder. Where depression is concerned, one major review found relaxation techniques were superior to no treatment at all, but not as effective as cognitive behavioral therapy.

Simply by helping you manage stress, the range of strategies outlined in this report may help prevent

Exploring the links between relaxation techniques and protective chemicals in the body

Can relaxation response techniques boost the production of certain substances that protect the body from illness and help stifle pain? Some evidence suggests that they can.

A team of Harvard Medical School researchers led by Dr. Jeffrey A. Dusek found that the relaxation response is associated with production of nitric oxide, a substance that offers a variety of health benefits. In this study, oxygen consumption and nitric oxide exhalation were measured in participants at the start of the trial, then again after eight weeks of training in evoking the relaxation response. While there was no correlation between the two measurements at the beginning of the program, by the end, oxygen consumption had decreased in proportion to an increase in nitric oxide production in the people who used the relaxation response. A control group showed no such change.

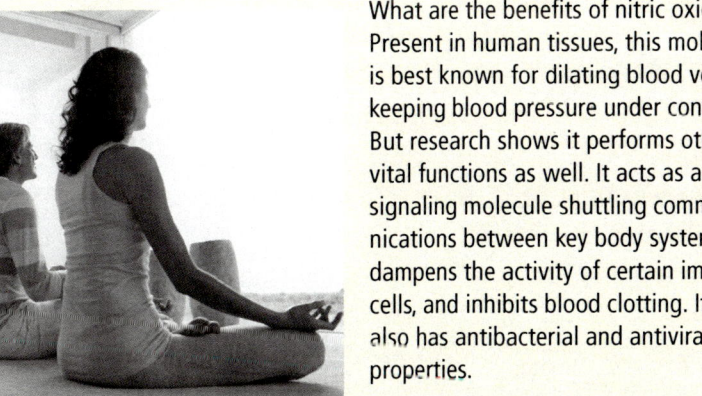

What are the benefits of nitric oxide? Present in human tissues, this molecule is best known for dilating blood vessels, keeping blood pressure under control. But research shows it performs other vital functions as well. It acts as a signaling molecule shuttling communications between key body systems, dampens the activity of certain immune cells, and inhibits blood clotting. It also has antibacterial and antiviral properties.

In fact, it stimulates activation of an enzyme that leads to the release of enkelytin, an antibacterial peptide, and enkephalins, compounds that enhance mood, reduce pain perception, and stimulate some immune system cells. To the researchers, this suggested that having sufficient levels of nitric oxide offers potential protection against microbes, health problems such as high blood pressure, and overzealous activity in the immune and vascular systems.

anxiety and depression, or bring you some relief from these problems. Distorted thoughts often fuel anxiety and depression, so it's likely that you'll find cognitive restructuring (see page 33) especially helpful.

Please note that it's also important to seek advice from a licensed mental health professional. After evaluating you, he or she may recommend a combination of medications and counseling, as well as a mind-body program or other stress management approaches.

Immune function

Studies suggest that the immune system is affected by both short-term sources of stress (such as academic exams or a fender-bender) and long-term sources (such as job strain or ongoing conflict with a spouse or partner). That said, the two types of stress may have different impacts on the immune system.

For example, short-term stress has been shown to boost the transfer of infection-fighting cells called lymphocytes from the bloodstream to the skin, which some researchers think could help block infection and enhance healing. Long-term stress, however, appears to have potentially harmful effects on certain immune cells. For example, natural killer cells, which attack virus-laden cells and certain tumor cells, may be suppressed by chronic stress. Viruses may also exploit vulnerability created by stress. Thus, you can wind up with more frequent—and more serious—bouts of colds and flu if your body feels the strain of chronic stress. What's more, wounds don't heal as quickly, and vaccines that might help you avoid certain ailments, such as flu, aren't as effective.

Once affected by stress, how swiftly does the immune system rebound? That depends on the source and duration of the stress, and on the individual. But worrisome changes in immune function have remained apparent for weeks and months following earthquakes and hurricanes. One study of current and former caregivers of spouses with Alzheimer's disease found that natural killer cells were significantly subdued among the caregivers compared with a control group. On average, this dampening of the immune system continued for three years after the role as caregiver ended.

Until the science of human immunity is more fully understood, however, the full effect of stress on the body's ability to resist disease remains uncertain.

Can stress management help?

It's too early to say. Certainly, lower levels of stress seem to translate to fewer colds and faster wound healing, which suggests improved immune function. However, low-grade, chronic inflammation—a type of immune response—contributes to many chronic ailments, and we don't know yet how stress management may affect all of them.

That said, an intriguing finding from the gene study mentioned previously (see "Genes and the relaxation response," page 6) is that the relaxation response temporarily switches off genes associated with chronic inflammatory responses in the body. Other research has shown that the relaxation reponse boosts levels of nitric oxide, which enhances some aspects of immune function (see "Exploring the links between relaxation techniques and protective chemicals in the body," page 13). Thus, it's possible, though not yet proven, that regularly practicing the relaxation response could help in healthful regulation of immune system activity.

Cancer

Cancer is not a single disease, but many diseases. What they have in common is the uncontrolled spread of abnormal cells. Currently, there is no evidence to suggest that stress causes cancer by itself. But whether long-term stress may play a role by tampering with immune defenses is a question that bears closer scrutiny. One theory about how cancer develops suggests that cancerous changes in cells occur frequently for a variety of reasons, but the immune system recognizes the cells as aberrant and destroys them. Only when the immune system becomes ineffective are the cancer cells able to multiply. Since chronic stress can hamper the immune system, this might affect the body's ability to head off the uncontrolled proliferation of cancerous cells.

Can stress management help?

It's too early to say whether managing stress affects the risk for various cancers. But there are promising hints. In 2008, Dr. Dean Ornish, president of the Preventive Medicine Research Institute in Sausalito, Calif., published a pilot study in the *Proceedings of the National Academy of Sciences*. The study participants were 30 men with early-stage, nonaggressive prostate cancer who had opted for "active surveillance" of their condition rather than medical treatment. They all agreed to go on Dr. Ornish's program, which combines a healthy low-fat diet with exercise, stress reduction techniques, and increased social support (which also reduces stress). In such a study, it's impossible to tell how great a role any of the four lifestyle interventions played individually. But the collective effect was impressive.

After three months on the program, an oncologist analyzed biopsy tissue taken from each of the men upon diagnosis and compared it with a second tissue sample taken after the three-month trial and found major changes in gene "expression"—that is, the activity of various genes. Across the board, the changes were of the type that can help protect against cancer and other major diseases. A total of 48 protective genes had become more active, including the "secreted frizzled-related protein" gene, which is a tumor suppressor. By contrast, 453 genes that promote inflammation, heart disease, and cancer were tamped down, including the RAN and SHOC2 genes, which are classified as tumor promoters. It was the first time anyone had shown that lifestyle changes may positively affect the genes involved in cancer. Of course, it's a long way from there to concluding that stress management can help prevent either the initiation or progression of cancer. Many more studies of greater size are needed.

At present, an interesting new line of inquiry is opening at the Benson-Henry Institute for Mind Body Medicine into multiple myeloma, an incurable cancer that affects blood cells. Certain gene changes found in multiple myeloma appear to be the opposite of gene changes evoked when healthy people elicit the relaxation response regularly (see "Genes and the relaxation response," page 6). Thus, it's possible that the relaxation response might beneficially act on pathways altered by multiple myeloma. The researchers are currently enrolling participants with asymptomo-

Can stress reduction slow aging?

There are tantalizing hints that learning to manage stress may even slow aging on the cellular level. Nobel Prize winner Elizabeth Blackburn of the University of California, San Francisco, has found that people under higher levels of stress tend to have shorter telomeres—the protective caps on the ends of chromosomes. That's important, because as telomeres shorten, cells die more quickly, and aging accelerates. One study that followed mothers of chronically ill children showed that those with the highest perceived stress levels had a dramatically shorter telomere length, indicating that their cells had aged an additional nine to 17 years compared with the normal aging pace of the low-stress group.

By contrast, a small 2013 study in *Lancet Oncology* from Blackburn and Dean Ornish found that after five years on Dr. Ornish's program of a low-fat diet, exercise, stress reduction, and social support, telomere length had increased by an average of 10% in the study's 10 active participants, versus a decrease of 3% in the 25 controls. Furthermore, there was a "dose response" effect, meaning that the greater the degree of positive lifestyle changes participants made, the greater the increases in their telomere length.

The results complement those of the 2013 gene study from the Benson-Henry Institute for Mind Body Medicine, which found that regularly eliciting the relaxation response leads to gene changes supporting telomeres (see "Genes and the relaxation response," page 6).

atic changes in blood cells that sometimes progress to multiple myeloma. The results remain to be seen.

In the meantime, it's clear that stress management can help people deal with some emotional and physical effects of cancer. According to the National Center for Complementary and Alternative Medicine, practicing mindfulness meditation can help relieve anxiety and stress in people with cancer, as well as ease fatigue and overall mood and sleep disturbances. And a small pilot study of men receiving radiation treatment for prostate cancer found that those who were anxious before the radiation treatment were less anxious after receiving one of two complementary treatments—relaxation response therapy or Reiki therapy. Those who received the relaxation response therapy also showed improvement in their sense of emotional well-being.

Figure 5: Provoking an asthma attack

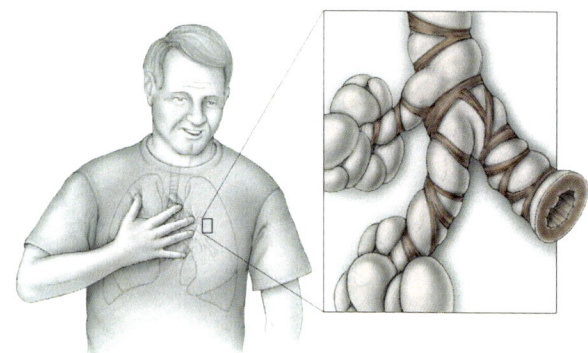

Stress can cause the small airways inside the lungs, known as bronchioles, to tighten. This constriction interferes with the flow of air into and out of your lungs. In people who are prone to asthma, this can trigger wheezing, breathlessness, and other symptoms of an asthma attack.

Asthma

Stress clearly plays a role in many cases of asthma. The bronchioles are small airways inside the lungs. Oxygen passing through them reaches air sacs called alveoli and is released into the bloodstream. Carbon dioxide from the blood collects in the alveoli and passes back through the bronchioles to be expelled by the lungs as you breathe out. But the autonomic nervous system constricts and dilates the bronchioles. Strong arousal can provoke bronchiole constriction, which makes it more difficult to move air in and out of the lungs. As a result, stress and strong emotions such as fear or anger commonly trigger asthma attacks (bouts of breathlessness and wheezing) in some people who have asthma (see Figure 5, at left). Of course, physical stressors, such as cold weather and exercise, can do the same.

The extent of stress's role in the development of asthma is still being debated. Intense family stress early in life has been proposed as one of several key risk factors. However, genetic predisposition, exposure to certain allergens, viral infections, and raised levels of certain allergy markers in the blood are also considered important.

Can stress management help?

It's too early to say. One small study published in *BMC Pulmonary Medicine* tested the effects of a yoga-based lifestyle modification and stress management program on 57 adults with mild or moderate bronchial asthma. The results showed a steady improvement in lung function, a decrease in exercise-induced airway constriction, improved quality of life as reported by participants, and a lower rate of medication use compared with a control group whose members received only physical care. However, more studies are needed. The National Center for Complementary and Alternative Medicine is currently funding research on whether mindfulness meditation could help people with asthma manage their symptoms or improve quality of life.

The different faces of stress

Perceptions of what constitutes a stressful situation and reactions to stress vary from person to person. Yet common factors play into the stress levels in our lives. Are you male or female? How old are you? Are you caring for an elderly or sick relative? Are you working (or do you wish you were)?

Gender and stress

The physiology of the stress response is similar for everyone. But some researchers believe you'll experience and respond to stress in distinctly different ways depending on whether you're a woman or man.

Community surveys taken in many countries find women consistently report greater distress than men do. A study of roughly 1,100 American adults that appeared in the *Journal of Personality and Social Psychology* found that women were more likely than men to experience ongoing stress and feel that their lives were out of their control. According to a national survey by the American Psychological Association, more women than men say they are under a great deal of stress. Also troubling, 49% of women surveyed reported that their stress has increased in the past five years, compared with 39% of men.

Why the disparities? Some researchers believe that the social responsibilities typically handled by women—including child care, care of older relatives, and housework—expose them to more abundant opportunities for distress. These responsibilities constitute the "second shift" for women who work outside the home—not to mention fodder for tension between intimate partners. This additional burden can lay the groundwork for long-term health problems. In one large study of nurses, women who were charged with caring for a disabled or chronically ill spouse for nine or more hours a week were at increased risk of having a heart attack or other manifestation of coronary artery disease over a four-year period.

Men, on the other hand, more often report financial stress than women do, which makes sense since men are traditionally expected to be the breadwinners. Another study asked 166 married couples to keep a daily diary tracking 21 common stressors, such as arguments and overloads at home and work, for a period of six weeks. Men reacted more strongly to financial woes, work overload, or an argument with a child, for example, while women were more distressed by arguments with a spouse, transportation difficulties, or family demands.

Men react more strongly to work overload and financial stress, while women are more stressed by family demands and transportation problems.

Some interesting research suggests that women and men also tend to cope with stressful situations in different ways. A team of UCLA psychologists published a study in *Psychological Review* finding that women are less likely to fight or flee when faced with stressors. Instead, they are likely to "tend-and-befriend." "Tending" is nurturing behavior designed to protect and relieve distress. "Befriending," which may support tending, refers to seeking and maintaining social connections. The researchers believe sex hormones and the pituitary hormone oxytocin are partly responsible for such differences and suggest the behavior may have held evolutionary advantages for women. Oxytocin dampens anxiety and induces

> **Tips for taming stress for older adults**

- ✔ Attend a mind-body program. Some are specifically designed for seniors. Others may focus on chronic pain or specific ailments, such as heart disease (see "Resources," page 52).
- ✔ Ask your doctor whether you might benefit from certain types of exercise, such as tai chi, which enhances balance, or strength training, which has been shown to build bone density and muscle strength in elderly people. Many other kinds of physical activity improve your health, lift your mood, and reduce stress, too.
- ✔ If insomnia is a considerable source of stress, cognitive behavioral therapy (CBT) may help. It aims to correct ingrained patterns of self-defeating behavior and negative thoughts. In a randomized, controlled study of 78 older adults published in *The Journal of the American Medical Association*, CBT was significantly more effective than sleep medication for improving insomnia over sustained periods. Ask your doctor to recommend a therapist or counselor who could help.
- ✔ If disability is a source of stress, talk with your doctor, a geriatrician, an occupational therapist, or a staff member at your local council on aging about changes in your home that might help you live more independently.
- ✔ Consider whether you might benefit from cognitive restructuring techniques or a course in assertiveness training that would help you state your wishes and handle conflicts.

relaxation. Some evidence suggests it heightens a sense of trust, too, possibly encouraging an impulse to reach out to others when distressed. It is intriguing to speculate on whether "tend-and-befriend" could have positive consequences for women. After all, social connections are key to reducing the damaging effects of stress (see "Social support," page 40). Interestingly, the effects of oxytocin are enhanced by female sex hormones and diminished by male sex hormones.

When under stress, both men and women release epinephrine and cortisol; men also release testosterone, which tends to increase hostility and aggression. For women, however, the impulse to fight or flee in the face of danger could have disastrous consequences, since they tend to be smaller than men and may be pregnant or caring for small children.

Aging and stress

Does your age have any effect on stress? Certainly some major life events, such as the death of a spouse or partner, illness, and accidents, are more likely to touch you with time. Ailments more common among older people, such as heart disease, arthritis, and cancer, are significant sources of pain and disability. Side effects from medications and other treatments can be unpleasant daily realities. Sleep disturbances are also common in later life. Any or all of these can be sources of stress.

A dwindling interest in exercise—tied, perhaps, to osteoporosis or compromised sight, hearing, and balance as you grow older—can make you more of a shut-in than you would like to be. This can set off a cycle of declining physical abilities and increasing frailty. Is that stressful? Just ask anyone who worries that a walk outside might end in broken bones or finds it difficult to do simple tasks around the house. People do adapt to changing abilities, it's true, but the road to that point may not be smooth.

Cultural training may make a difference, too. Many older people were raised in environments where emotional displays were frowned upon. Many older women never learned how to state needs directly or handle uncomfortable conflicts before they become a source of stress; nor did they have abundant opportunities for work outside the home, which offers a creative, productive outlet to some women. On the other hand, many do take comfort from religion, which may have an effect on health and longevity.

Some preliminary evidence suggests that disturbances in the HPA axis, which controls the stress response, compound certain health problems that are common among older people, such as cardiovascular disease and stroke. Aging and long-term stress both appear to trigger these disturbances in some people. Constant exposure to certain stress hormones, such as cortisol, can harm nerve cells in the brain region known as the hippocampus, potentially affecting learning and memory processing.

Fortunately, not all of these consequences are inevitable. Once you identify key sources of stress in your life, odds are good that you can overcome them. It's possible to prevent or at least combat physical decline and some age-related ailments through exercise, good nutrition, appropriate medications, and stress control techniques. (Also try the "Tips for taming stress for older adults," page 18.)

Teens and stress

As any parent can tell you, teens—and even "tweens"—are feeling the effects of stress in record numbers. What many parents might not realize is how strongly their own stress affects their children: children who say their parents always seem stressed are eight times as likely to report stress themselves as children who say their parents never seem stressed, according to a national survey from the American Psychological Association. An upsurge in certain parental behaviors—like yelling, arguing, and complaining—tip off children that parents feel worried or stressed.

So, other than parents, what stresses teens in particular? High on the list are academic pressures, especially among students who hope to go to college; social pressures (think of friends, romance, and bullies); and worry about the future. Teens who report feeling under stress often experience physical symptoms, such as headaches, stomach upset, and trouble sleeping. Depression, anxiety, upticks in violent behavior (like lashing out at others physically), and even suicide are possible consequences, too.

Just like adults, teens may manage their stress in a variety of ways. At this stage in life, their coping skills aren't necessarily positive. The top three coping strategies reported by the APA are listening to music (66%), watching TV (34%), and playing video games (30%). Although this sounds fairly benign, these are sedentary activities with poor implications for overall health. Substance abuse, binge eating or not eating, and cutting themselves with razors or other shap objects are more worrisome choices made by some teens seeking stress relief.

Marilyn Wilcher, author of *Grab a Tiger by the Toe: Stress-Proof Your Child*, directs the Education Initiative at the Benson-Henry Institute for Mind Body Medicine, which works with schools on stress management programs for children of all ages. "Teaching teens relaxation response techniques and other stress management tools builds their resiliency and sense of control," she says. "Learning these skills now gives them positive coping strategies for life."

One study at the Benson-Henry Institute tested the feasibility of a four-week, eight-session curriculum for high school students combining relaxation

▶ Tips for taming teen stress

IF YOU'RE A TEEN:

- ✔ You can easily learn relaxation response techniques (see "Managing your stress through the relaxation response," page 24). The two simple steps spelled out in that section work well when you're sitting quietly and comfortably, or while you're running, swimming, or walking, since repetitive activities help put you in a relaxed state.
- ✔ Mini-relaxations take as little as 15 to 60 seconds (see "Try a mini-relaxation," page 47).
- ✔ As soon as you start to feel stressed, try taking a few deep, belly breaths (see "Breath focus," page 25).
- ✔ Imagine success. If you have an exam coming up, put yourself in the picture as you meditate by imagining yourself acing the test (see "Guided imagery," page 28, for tips on this).

IF YOU'RE A PARENT:

- ✔ Remember that your behavior when under stress affects your teen. Managing your own stress may actually decrease the amount of stress your teen feels—and you're providing an excellent role model to follow.
- ✔ Work with your child to learn the tools needed to stop, breathe, reflect, and choose (see page 34) when negative thoughts send stress skyrocketing ("I'm terrible at math; I'm bound to flunk this test"; "My best friend isn't answering my texts; she must be furious with me"). Practicing together could be helpful to you both.
- ✔ At dinner, go around the table asking everyone to share one good thing that happened during their day. Simple pleasures, kind acts, and personal victories all qualify: "I have three new followers on Instagram," "I forgot to bring lunch and my friend shared his with me," or "I got an A on my bio project." This reinforces positive feelings.

exercises, tenets of positive psychology, and skills to help recognize and reframe negative thoughts. Reporting in the *Journal of Adolescence* in 2011, the researchers noted that the curriculum prompted positive changes in perceived stress, anxiety, and health-promoting behaviors, particularly among teenage girls.

Caregiving and stress

Caring for others fulfills a basic social contract in ways that can draw generations and individuals closer to one another. Certainly, caring for an elderly parent or ailing spouse or partner is a worthy, often satisfying pursuit. But it isn't easy. If you're among the estimated 66 million Americans acting as caregivers for friends, family, or neighbors, you may often wrestle with stress as well as exhaustion, anger, guilt, grief, and other difficult emotions.

Two-thirds of these caregivers are women. The task is especially hard on women in the so-called sandwich generation, who are simultaneously caring for children and older parents, quite possibly while working outside the home, too.

While you attend to the needs of others, your own sense of well-being may head south. Studies of men and women responsible for the long-term care of relatives show higher rates of illness, suppressed immune response, slower healing, and even increased mortality among caregivers. Additionally, research reveals that ongoing stress endured by older adults caring for spouses with Alzheimer's disease has a negative impact on the caregiver's own mental functioning.

In order to give care to others, you need stress relief, support, and time for yourself and your family. The "Tips for taming caregiver stress," below, may help.

▶ Tips for taming caregiver stress

- ✔ Relaxation response techniques and nurturing techniques (see "Nurturing yourself," page 42) are vital. Practicing them often will enable you to feel calmer, happier, and better able to help others. If it's too hard to find the time, consider getting extra help with some household tasks. (The Eldercare Locator at www.eldercare.gov can help you find varied services for older adults and their families; it's run by the Administration on Aging.)

- ✔ Protect your own health. Research suggests that a caregiver's immune function is often suppressed by the stress of caring for others. Boost your resistance by eating well, getting enough rest and exercise, and pursuing activities that bring you pleasure. Take advantage of regular respite care from professionals, family, and friends to give you much-needed breaks.

- ✔ Join a support group to talk out frustrations with other people in your situation and to get helpful ideas. Some caregiver support groups are available online (such as a nationwide chat group run by AARP), while others are run by local hospitals, senior centers, and community groups.

- ✔ A blend of assertiveness and cognitive restructuring skills can help you share the work, instead of taking on everything yourself. Spell out to other family members what needs to be done and what sort of help would be best. If no one offers help, ask for it. Linking to those who can lend a hand has gotten much easier with new websites and apps that help friends, family, and communities coordinate care. Two examples of helpful sites are www.lotsahelpinghands.com and also www.caringbridge.org.

- ✔ When someone offers help, accept. Keep handy a list of small tasks people can do, such as calling regularly, cooking an occasional dinner, shopping, and running errands. You can dole out tasks or ask people to check off what they can do.

- ✔ Online message boards for caregivers allow people to chat with experts, or post questions and get communal responses. AARP runs one such helpful site (a quick link to it is at www.health.harvard.edu/cgteam). Another online resource with excellent coverage on a range of caregiving topics is the New Old Age blog of *The New York Times* (http://newoldage.blogs.nytimes.com).

- ✔ Accept that circumstances change quickly. Periodically, consider what you can offer and what assistance you need. If it's getting too hard to fulfill certain needs, ask family members for help or consider other options, such as hiring paid caregivers to take on these tasks. Consult a geriatric care manager (www.caremanager.org) or social worker for help; your local council on aging or visiting nurse association should be able to help you find one. If necessary, consider another living arrangement that would help you meet your needs and those of your loved one.

Work and stress

Americans spend long hours working. In recent decades, cellphones, telecommuting, email, and fax machines have breached the wall between work and leisure time. Frequent threats of layoffs and the flight of industries to markets where labor is cheaper fuel worker worries. The jobs of older workers may be jeopardized by younger aspirants who are well-versed in new technologies or simply less costly to a corporation. A generally shaky economy and the rise in food and gas prices also feed anxiety.

Given this picture, is work-related stress increasing? It's hard to be certain. Some researchers have pointed out that the scales designed to measure stress at work may be too narrow to fit people in a wide range of occupations and aren't always applicable to current work practices. In addition, beneficial changes, such as the elimination of some dirty, tedious jobs and a growth in opportunities available in challenging new fields, generally get little attention. So do the positive psychological effects of work.

Perhaps a better question, then, is how does your job affect you? Does it engage and energize you or leave you sapped? Does it satisfy you? Do you get the support you need to do your job? How much control do you have over your work? A study of almost 21,300 female registered nurses found those reporting minimal control over their jobs, little social support at work, and high job demands were more likely to be in poor health when data collection started. They also suffered greater functional declines during the next four years. In this study, published in *BMJ*, job control depended on the worker's ability to acquire and apply new skills on the job and to have decision-making authority. Women in jobs with the highest control and lowest demands stayed healthiest.

Another study, which involved 10,000 London-based male and female civil servants, linked job stress and heart disease. The researchers found that chronic work stress was associated with coronary artery disease, especially among people under age 50.

No matter how you rate your job, you can find ways to defuse the stress response whenever work triggers it. Start by trying the "Tips for taming work-related stress," above right.

Tips for taming work-related stress

✔ Try a mini-relaxation (see page 47) for fast relief.

✔ Halt cognitive distortions before they get too strong a toehold. Remember to stop, breathe, reflect, and choose (see page 34).

✔ Take a 10-minute break for a body scan (see page 27) on days when tension builds up.

✔ Practice self-nurturing techniques at work as well as outside of it. Buy flowers for your desk, have lunch with your favorite co-workers, or go for a short walk.

✔ Practice mindfulness (see "Use mindfulness to reduce workday stress," page 48).

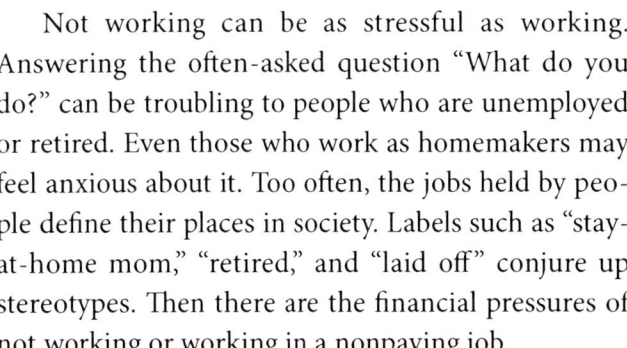

Not working can be as stressful as working. Answering the often-asked question "What do you do?" can be troubling to people who are unemployed or retired. Even those who work as homemakers may feel anxious about it. Too often, the jobs held by people define their places in society. Labels such as "stay-at-home mom," "retired," and "laid off" conjure up stereotypes. Then there are the financial pressures of not working or working in a nonpaying job.

You can counter these stressors in many ways. Addressing cognitive distortions and exaggerations can help you manage realistic and unrealistic fears (see "Cognitive restructuring," page 33). Practicing relaxation and self-nurturing techniques will lower your stress levels. Websites and bookstores are filled with career advice ranging from identifying the work you love to acing job interviews. Be aware, too, that there is a life beyond work where satisfaction and opportunity exist (see "Creativity, productivity, and leisure," page 42).

What about stress in *your* life?

In the course of a lifetime, odds are good that you'll survive some very stressful events. You'll also face a gamut of far smaller day-to-day stressors. But do you even realize the effects these are having? The checklist below will help you recognize your personal stress warning signs.

Once you're aware of how stress makes you feel and act, you can use the many different tools described in the second half of this report to help quell its effects. Before turning to this, though, consider whether you typically choose healthy or unhealthy responses to stress and find out more about how the connection of mind and body may harm—and help—you.

Healthy vs. unhealthy responses to stress

You probably have your own ways of dealing with

▶ My stress warning signs

Being able to recognize when you're feeling stressed can help you quickly counteract the stress response. A good first step is to look over the list below and check off all the symptoms you recognize.

Physical symptoms
- ☐ Tight neck and shoulders
- ☐ Back pain
- ☐ Sleep difficulties
- ☐ Tiredness or fatigue
- ☐ Racing heartbeat or palpitations
- ☐ Shakiness or tremors
- ☐ Sweating
- ☐ Ringing in ears
- ☐ Dizziness or fainting
- ☐ Choking sensation
- ☐ Difficulty swallowing
- ☐ Stomachache
- ☐ Indigestion
- ☐ Diarrhea or constipation
- ☐ Frequent, urgent need to urinate
- ☐ Loss of interest in sex
- ☐ Restlessness

Behavioral symptoms
- ☐ Grinding of teeth
- ☐ Inability to complete tasks
- ☐ Overly critical attitude
- ☐ Bossiness
- ☐ Fidgeting
- ☐ Overuse of alcohol
- ☐ Emotional eating or overeating
- ☐ Fist clenching
- ☐ Changes in the amount of alcohol or food you consume
- ☐ Taking up smoking or smoking more than usual
- ☐ Increased desire to be with or withdraw from others
- ☐ Rumination (frequent talking or brooding about stressful situations)

Emotional symptoms
- ☐ Crying
- ☐ Irritability
- ☐ Edginess
- ☐ Anger
- ☐ Boredom
- ☐ Nervousness
- ☐ Feeling anxious
- ☐ Quick temper
- ☐ Lack of meaning in life and pursuits
- ☐ Loneliness
- ☐ Unhappiness with no clear cause
- ☐ Depression
- ☐ Feeling powerless to change things

Cognitive symptoms
- ☐ Continual worry
- ☐ Poor concentration
- ☐ Trouble remembering things
- ☐ Loss of sense of humor
- ☐ Indecisiveness
- ☐ Lack of creativity
- ☐ Trouble thinking clearly

Other symptoms
_____
_____
_____
_____
_____
_____

stressful times. Some may be healthy, such as calling a friend, treating yourself to a massage, or curling up in bed earlier than usual. Others may not be as helpful. All too often, people self-medicate or turn to other unhealthy behaviors in an attempt to relieve pressure they feel. They may do so in a variety of ways.

For example, less healthy responses to stress include the following:
- watching endless hours of TV
- withdrawing from friends or partners or, conversely, jumping into a frenzied social life to avoid facing problems
- overeating or weight gain
- undereating or weight loss
- sleeping too much
- drinking too much alcohol
- lashing out at others in emotionally or physically violent outbursts
- smoking, or smoking more than usual
- taking prescription or over-the-counter drugs that promise some form of relief, such as sleeping pills, muscle relaxants, or anti-anxiety pills
- taking illegal or unsafe drugs.

Becoming aware of how you typically handle stress can help you make healthy choices. If you normally reach for a sugary snack, for example, you might instead call a friend. Choosing to connect rather than consume can relieve your stress. Studies suggest that emphasizing social ties can provide definite health benefits, too—with no calories!

Managing your stress through the relaxation response

In the late 1970s, working in the very same room at Harvard Medical School where Walter B. Cannon first delved into the biochemistry of stress, cardiologist Herbert Benson launched landmark research into the health hazards of stress and the body's counterbalancing potential for self-healing. Since that time, Dr. Benson and many other researchers have investigated the stress response and its antidotes—the relaxation response and the other stress management strategies described in this section and the next.

Dr. Benson is the medical editor of this report and director emeritus of the Benson-Henry Institute for Mind Body Medicine, which advises using a combination of approaches for stress management. Among these healthy self-care strategies are

- learning various techniques that elicit the relaxation response, such as breath focus and guided imagery
- using cognitive restructuring, a method of helping you reframe negative thoughts in order to cope more effectively with a difficult situation
- nurturing yourself by exercising regularly, eating healthy foods, pursuing activities that add joy to your life, and setting aside time for socializing, relaxing, and connecting with others.

Self-care strategies like these can make an enormous difference to your health and well-being.

Cardiovascular disease offers an excellent example. Research shows that regularly evoking the relaxation response leads to lasting declines in high blood pressure. Stress management techniques that short-circuit the stress response, such as reframing negative or runaway thoughts, can also reduce blood pressure. Good nutrition and regular exercise can improve levels of cholesterol, as well as blood pressure. Social support also has a strong protective effect on heart health. Over time, the combination of these self-care approaches may ward off serious consequences and reduce or possibly even eliminate the need for certain medications.

Eliciting the relaxation response

Two simple steps. That's all it takes to elicit the relaxation response, a deep physiologic shift in the body that is the opposite of the stress response. Try these two steps anytime you feel stressed in order to regain a sense of calm and peace.

■ **Step 1: Choose a calming focus.** Good examples are your breath, a sound ("Om"), a short prayer, or a positive word (such as "relax" or "peace") or phrase ("breathing in calm, breathing out tension"; "I am relaxed"). Repeat this aloud or silently as you inhale or exhale.

■ **Step 2: Let go and relax.** Don't worry about how you're doing. When you notice your mind has wandered, simply take a deep breath or say to yourself "thinking, thinking" and gently return your attention to your focus.

The relaxation response puts the brakes on the runaway biological changes that put us into overdrive. By carving out 10 to 20 minutes daily to practice techniques that elicit the relaxation response, you can help reduce the cumulative effects of stress on your body.

> "Think of modern health care as a sturdy, three-legged stool. Two of these approaches—medication and medical procedures—are invaluable. Yet when used alone, they form only two legs of the stool. Proven self-care approaches are the stabilizing third leg."
>
> —Dr. Herbert Benson, director emeritus of the Benson-Henry Institute for Mind Body Medicine

A number of physiological changes occur during the relaxation response. Heartbeat and breathing slow down. The body uses less oxygen, and blood flows more easily throughout the circulatory network of veins and arteries. Blood lactate levels, which some researchers believe are linked with anxiety attacks, decline markedly.

You can elicit the relaxation response in many other ways, too, including these:
- breath focus (see below, right)
- body scan (see page 27)
- guided imagery (see page 28)
- mindfulness meditation (see page 29)
- yoga, tai chi, or qigong (see page 30)
- repetitive prayer (see page 31).

Of course, these are not the only techniques that can help you elicit the relaxation response. You may find others that are quite effective. What's crucial is that the method you choose interrupts the train of everyday thoughts by letting you focus on a word, phrase, prayer, or repetitive activity. Once you learn these techniques, you can practice them regularly almost anywhere. No special equipment or expert trainer is required, although many people find mind-body programs, relaxation response CDs, and meditation or yoga classes helpful as they learn a new technique (see "Resources," page 52).

Rather than choosing just one technique to elicit the relaxation response, we recommend sampling many. Some methods are bound to work better for you than others. If your favorite fails to engage you at times, you'll have an alternative. And many people get the best results from combining several techniques.

Embracing a routine
Whether you are trying to lose weight, exercise more, or teach your body to relax, establishing a new behavior can be challenging at first. Establishing a routine for relaxation response sessions will help you make your new behavior stick. Follow these tips:
- Practice regularly, once or twice a day. Choosing a particular time of day can enhance the sense of ritual, which will enable you to practice more easily. Many people choose to use relaxation techniques in the morning before breakfast, since it can be hard to schedule time later in the day. Evidence suggests the more regularly you use these techniques, the better the outcome.
- Aim for at least 10 to 20 minutes daily. You might do this in one sitting, or try several five-minute segments spaced throughout the day. If you're pressed for time, remember that any time spent eliciting the relaxation response and practicing mini-relaxation techniques (see "Try a mini-relaxation," page 47) is better for your mind and body than none.

Relaxing the brain

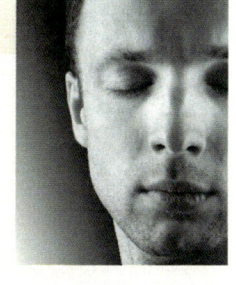

A small study of five subjects used functional magnetic resonance imaging (fMRI) to map the parts of the brain that are active during meditation sessions that induce the relaxation response. Although overall brain activity declined, signals increased in areas of the brain involved in attention as well as arousal and control of the autonomic nervous system.

This suggests that meditation induces deep relaxation, yet sparks intense neural activity because of the vigilance required to keep the mind from wandering. By shining light on observable biological changes triggered by the relaxation response, this study helps bolster the concept that it is a distinct state and may also build support for its use in modern health care.

Breath focus
Breath focus is a simple yet powerful technique that can elicit the relaxation response for people of different backgrounds. Occasionally, however, health problems or anxiety may make using this technique uncomfortable (see Table 1, page 26). The first step to practicing breath focus is learning to breathe deeply from the diaphragm.

The importance of deep breathing
Watch a baby breathe and you'll notice that the infant's belly expands and contracts naturally with each deep, powerful breath. By contrast, most adults tend to take shallow breaths—and fill only their upper lungs, so that their chests rise—when told to breathe deeply. We could all take a lesson from our children. When you breathe deeply—a practice called diaphragmatic

breathing, abdominal breathing, or belly breathing—the air coming in through your nose fills both your upper and lower lungs rather than only the upper portion. Compared with the shallow, quick breaths you take when panic strikes, deep, diaphragmatic breathing feels very calming.

Try it for a few moments right now. First, place one hand on your chest with fingers comfortably apart. Now place your other hand just below your belly button. As you breathe deeply in and out, you should notice that your lower belly rises and falls. When you breathe more shallowly—which feels normal to many people—only your chest rises. Reawakening your inborn ability to breathe abdominally allows you to tap one of your body's strongest self-healing mechanisms.

Each time you breathe you engage the diaphragm, a strong sheet of muscle that separates your chest from your abdomen (see Figure 6, page 27). As you breathe in, the diaphragm drops downward, pulling your lungs with it and pressing against abdominal organs to make room for your lungs to expand as they fill with air. As you breathe out, the diaphragm presses back upward against your lungs, helping to expel carbon dioxide. However, shallow breathing hobbles the diaphragm's range of motion. The lowest portion of the lungs—where many small blood vessels instrumental in carrying oxygen to cells reside—never gets a full share of oxygenated air, making you feel anxious and short of breath.

By contrast, deep abdominal breathing encourages full oxygen exchange—that is, the beneficial trade of incoming oxygen for outgoing carbon dioxide. Not surprisingly, this type of breathing slows the heartbeat and can lower or stabilize blood pressure (see "High blood pressure," page 10).

Table 1: Which technique is right for you?

By regularly practicing techniques that elicit the relaxation response, you create a well of calm to dip into as the need arises. As this chart details, these techniques can be especially beneficial under certain circumstances, but may not be suitable under others.

METHOD	WHAT IS IT?	ESPECIALLY BENEFICIAL	MAY NOT BE SUITABLE
Breath focus	Focusing on slow, deep breathing and gently disengaging the mind from distracting thoughts and sensations	If you have an eating disorder or tend to hold in your stomach; may help you focus on your body in healthier ways	If you have health problems that make breathing difficult, such as respiratory ailments or heart failure, or if you suffer from anxiety and panic attacks
Body scan	Focusing on one part of the body or group of muscles at a time and mentally releasing any physical tension you feel there	For increasing your awareness of the mind-body connection	If you have had a recent surgery that affects body image or other difficulties with body image
Guided imagery	Using pleasing mental images to help you relax and focus	When you want to reinforce a positive vision of yourself or a goal you wish to reach	If you have intrusive thoughts that make imagery difficult; if you have difficulty with visualizations
Mindfulness meditation	Breathing deeply while staying in the moment by deliberately focusing on thoughts and sensations that arise during the meditation session	If racing thoughts make other forms of meditation difficult	If you find it too hard to commit the needed time
Yoga, tai chi, and qigong	Three ancient arts that combine rhythmic breathing with a series of postures or flowing movements	At times when your mind is racing; whenever you find it especially hard to settle down and focus; if you wish to enhance flexibility and balance	If you are not normally active or have health problems or a painful or disabling condition that might make these activities difficult; check with your doctor before starting
Repetitive prayer	Using a short prayer or phrase from a prayer to help enhance breath focus	If religion or spirituality is meaningful to you	If you are not religious

Practicing breath focus

Breath focus is quite simple to do.

- Find a comfortable, quiet place to sit or lie down and start by observing your breath. First take a normal breath. Then try taking a slow, deep breath. Picture the air coming in through your nose moving downward, deep into your lungs. Let your abdomen expand fully. Now breathe out through your mouth (or your nose, if that feels more natural).
- Alternate normal and deep breaths several times. Pay attention to how you feel when you inhale and exhale normally and when you breathe deeply. Shallow breathing often feels tense and constricted, while deep breathing produces relaxation.
- Now practice deep, diaphragmatic breathing for several minutes. Put one hand on your abdomen, just below your belly button. Feel your hand rise about an inch each time you inhale and fall about an inch each time you exhale. Your chest will rise slightly, too, in concert with your abdomen. Remember to relax your belly so that each inhalation expands it fully.

Once you've taken the steps above, you can move on to regular practice of breath focus.

- As you sit comfortably with your eyes closed, blend your breathing with helpful imagery and use a focus word or phrase that will help you relax.
- Imagine that the air you breathe in washes peace and calm into your body.
- As you breathe out, imagine that the air leaving your body carries tension and anxiety away with it.
- Try saying these phrases silently to yourself: "Breathing in peace and calm" on the inhale and "Breathing out tension and anxiety" on the exhale.

Initially, 10 minutes of breath focus is a reasonable goal. Gradually add time until your sessions are about 15 to 20 minutes long.

Body scan

A body scan is a relaxation technique that blends breath focus and visualization with progressive muscle relaxation. This technique helps you become more attuned to your body and aware of the connection between your mind and body.

Almost everyone carries unnecessary tension in his or her muscles. But where each of us feels it varies. One woman might have a tight neck and shoulders, while her husband feels an iron band digging into his forehead. A body scan can help you locate—and release—the tension in your body.

Figure 6: What happens as you breathe

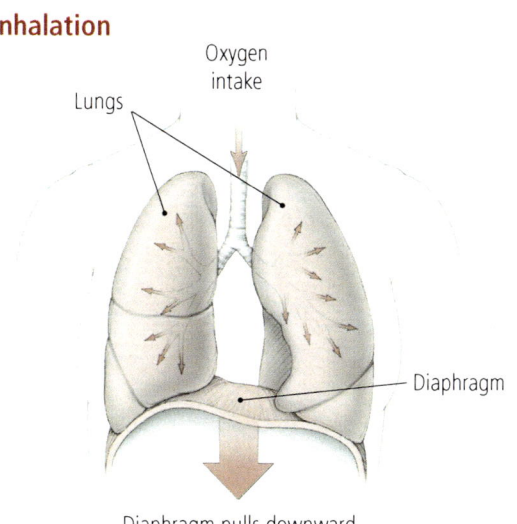

Inhalation

Diaphragm pulls downward, helping lungs expand with oxygen

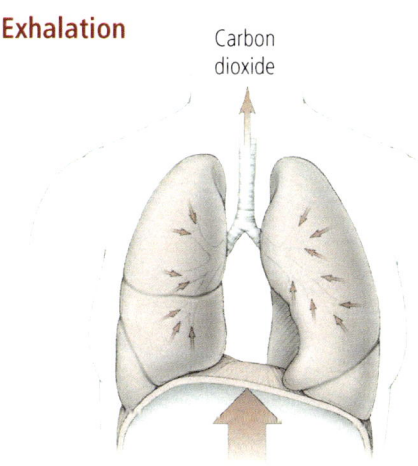

Exhalation

Diaphragm returns upward, forcing lungs to expel carbon dioxide

Learning to breathe abdominally is the first step in practicing breath focus, a stress management technique that elicits the relaxation response. As you breathe in, your diaphragm drops, giving your lungs the room they need to expand. If you are breathing properly, you should feel your lungs fill completely and your chest and belly expand. As you exhale, your diaphragm pushes up against your lungs, which helps to expel the carbon dioxide.

Practicing the body scan

Performing a body scan is quite simple. Concentrate on one part of your body at a time. As you do, picture that muscle in your mind. Imagine it open, warm, and relaxed. Feel any tension melt away. As a guide, use these steps, which are adapted from the book *Mind Your Heart* by Dr. Herbert Benson and Aggie Casey:

- Choose a comfortable spot to sit or lie down, closing your eyes. Begin with two minutes of breath focus. Take slow, deep breaths, allowing your stomach to rise as you inhale and fall as you exhale.
- Next, concentrate on your right big toe. Imagine the atoms in your toe and focus on the space between each atom. Imagine your toe feeling open, warm, and relaxed.
- Now shift your focus to each of the other toes on your right foot, visualizing them one by one. Again, notice the sensations of your toes and envision them as open, warm, and relaxed.
- Slowly shift your focus to your foot, moving mentally from the ball of your foot to the arch, then the top of the foot.
- Now work your way up your right leg, turning your attention to your ankle, calf, knee, thigh, and hip. Take your time, slowly working through each area. For each body part, envision the atoms and the space between those atoms. Picture each muscle feeling open, warm, and relaxed.
- Allow your right leg to relax, sinking into the support of the floor.
- Now repeat these steps, focusing on your left foot and leg.
- Next, become aware of your back. Does it feel tight or tense? Pay attention to each vertebra and the space that surrounds it. Let each vertebra feel light and spacious. Slowly work your way up your back, relaxing each muscle there.
- Gradually, move on to your abdomen and chest. Picture your organs and the space between them. Allow your belly to feel light and open.
- Become aware of your right thumb, and then your remaining fingers. Envision each finger one by one, then slowly work your way through your hand and arm: relax your palm, wrist, forearm, elbow, upper arm, and shoulder.
- Feel your right arm relax and feel warm, spacious, and light.
- Do the same thing with your left hand and arm.
- Think about your neck and jaw. Yawn. Allow each part of your face to relax, working through your jaw, eyes, and forehead. Shift your attention to the top and back of your head.
- Let your whole body sink into your chair or bed. Does it feel light and relaxed? Focus on your breath. Imagine yourself breathing in calm and peace. As you breathe out, imagine any remaining tension being expelled from your body.
- If any part of your body is still tense, focus on that area, releasing tension from that spot as you exhale.
- Sit or lie quietly for a few minutes, noting how light and spacious your body feels. Then open your eyes slowly. Take a moment to stretch, if you'd like.

Guided imagery

Conjuring soothing scenes through guided imagery, or visualization, can be a powerful way of evoking the relaxation response. The images you choose—whether scenes, places, or experiences—enhance your sensation of inner calm and help break the chain of everyday thought. While imagery is often touted as beneficial for people with cancer or other illnesses, not enough studies support some of the health-enhancing claims. It has, however, been shown to

▶ Blue dots

A visual reminder can help you short-circuit stress. Blue dots—which you can buy in packets at any stationery or office supply store—do the trick quite nicely. Where should you put them? Any place where your stress meter tends to swing upward: on a car dashboard in readiness for traffic jams, near your work phone or computer, and maybe on the refrigerator or a cabinet where sweets are stashed.

Let the blue dot remind you to stop and breathe, while putting a halt to negative thoughts or distortions (see "Recognizing your distortions," page 34); carve out time for the relaxation response; reach out to a friend; try a mini-relaxation (see page 47); or simply take a few deep, calming breaths till the traffic light turns green.

lessen pain and the side effects of various drugs, including chemotherapy.

Lush descriptions of sandy beaches, bubbling streams, and fields of flowers that help people visualize calming scenes can be recorded or are available for free or a fee as downloads, CDs, or YouTube videos. Just be sure that the imagery you choose is soothing to you and has personal significance, because the exercise won't be effective otherwise. For example, a field of flowers could have negative associations if you suffer from hay fever.

Practicing guided imagery

Before you start your guided imagery session, find a quiet place to sit.

- Arrange your body comfortably. Clear your mind while taking deep, even breaths for several minutes.
- If you aren't using recorded imagery, conjure up your own safe or special haven (perhaps a lake cabin, a beach house, your grandmother's kitchen, or a garden) and imagine yourself there.
- Allow all of your senses to be present. What do you smell—pine needles, rain steaming off hot pavement, vanilla in the kitchen? What do you hear and see? Are clouds or birds passing by? Drink in the surrounding colors. Concentrate on sensory pleasures: a cool breeze on your cheek, gravel crunching underfoot, or the scent of flowering trees.
- Accept intrusive thoughts passively by observing them but not reacting to them. Then return to your focus. Practice for 10 to 20 minutes. (Also see "Harness the power of your mind," page 48, for some longer guided imagery scripts you can try.)

Mindfulness meditation

In our busy world, multitasking is a way of life. We fold the laundry while keeping one eye on the kids and another on the television. We chat on our cell phones while commuting to work. We pay the bills, munch on a snack, and listen to a spouse or partner complain about a work project, all at the same time. But in the rush to accomplish necessary tasks, we often lose our connection with the present moment. We sprint through daily activities without being truly attentive to what we're doing and how we're feeling.

In contrast, mindfulness, which has its roots in Buddhist practices, teaches us to live each moment as it unfolds. Rather than juggling tasks, you attend to just one at a time. Mindfulness is the practice of focusing attention on what is happening in the present and accepting it without judgment. And that—many physicians and therapists believe—can be a powerful therapeutic tool.

Mindfulness is often learned through meditation, a method of regulating your attention by focusing on your breathing, a phrase, or an image. Scientists have discovered the benefits of using mindfulness meditation techniques to help relieve stress, treat heart disease, and alleviate conditions such as high blood pressure, chronic pain, sleep problems, and gastrointestinal difficulties.

Therapists—particularly cognitive behavioral therapists—have turned to mindfulness techniques to treat mood problems. Studies have found that mindfulness meditation can help prevent relapse in people who have had several episodes of depression. There is evidence that meditation has distinct effects on the brain. In one study, researchers measured brain electrical activity before, immediately after, and four months after a two-month course in mindfulness meditation. They found persistent increased activity on the left side of the prefrontal cortex, which is associated with joyful and serene emotions.

Mindfulness offers other benefits. It enhances your appreciation of simple everyday experiences. By learning to focus on the here and now, many people who practice mindfulness find that they are less likely to get caught up in worries about the future or regrets over the past.

Mindfulness meditation teaches you to focus on distracting thoughts and sensations that occur. Some experts in the field—such as Jon Kabat-Zinn, author of *Full Catastrophe Living* and founder of the Stress Reduction Clinic at the University of Massachusetts Medical Center—believe that facing what arises and opening yourself up to it is the first step toward personal transformation and growth.

A resiliency toolbox: Empower yourself in the face of stress

Why is it that two people in the exact same situation—perhaps hearing that their flight is late—can react in dramatically different ways? While one person yells, curses, and stomps his feet, his friend stops, takes a breath, and calmly gathers information about the other possible transportation options. Although neither has the power to make the flight depart on time, both can control how they perceive the situation and how well they cope.

Simply put, your wellness depends on both the total amount of stress in your life (over which you may have little or no control) and your ability to deal with it. But you have a resiliency toolbox (over which you do have control) into which you can add various tools and techniques for handling stressful events.

Fortunately, you have tremendous power to sharpen your resiliency tools and expand your coping repertoire. Learning to elicit the relaxation response, stopping negative or runaway thoughts that trigger the stress response, learning how to communicate calmly and effectively, and developing social bonds are some of the many tools you can use to change the way you perceive and respond to stressors. It is never too late to heed your personal warning signs of stress and to learn how to better manage challenging or stressful events in a calmer, healthier way. By doing so, you can reduce the negative effects of stress—such as higher blood pressure—on your physical health, as well as improve your emotional health. You might find that your relationships with others benefit as well.

Practicing mindfulness meditation

Here's how to get started with mindfulness meditation.
- Sit on a straight-backed chair or cross-legged on the floor. Focus on an aspect of your breathing, such as the sensations of air flowing into your nostrils and out of your mouth, or your belly rising and falling as you inhale and exhale.
- Once you've narrowed your concentration in this way, begin to widen your focus. Become aware of sounds, sensations, and ideas. Embrace and consider each without judgment. If your mind starts to race, return your focus to your breathing.
- Then expand your awareness again. Kabat-Zinn recommends committing to 45 minutes of meditation at least six days a week without expectations, but if time is limited, try a 20-minute session daily.

A less formal approach to mindfulness can also encourage you to stay in the present and truly participate in your life. You can choose any task or moment to practice mindfulness. Whether you are eating, showering, walking, touching a partner, or playing with a child or grandchild, attending to these three points will help:
- Start with breath focus and return to it periodically, staying aware of each inhalation and exhalation.
- Proceed with the task or pleasure at hand slowly and with full deliberation.
- Engage your senses fully so that you savor every sensation.

Peeling and eating an orange offers an excellent example. For a few moments, just concentrate on your breath moving in and out of your nostrils. Look at the orange, turning it over in your hands. Run your fingertips over its bumpy texture and absorb its vibrant color and light citrus scent. As you peel it, engage your senses fully. Note the slight spray as your fingers dig into and peel back the hardened skin and soft white pith. How does the orange smell and feel now? Are you salivating? When you put a slice of it into your mouth and break through the thin membrane into its juicy center, what sensations do you feel? Savor the taste.

Try not to hurry through one mouthful of orange to get to the next. Slow down and stay in the moment. Before you swallow each portion of the orange, be aware of the rising desire to do so. Then note how it feels when you swallow. Throughout the experience, remain fully aware. How much are you eating? How do you feel physically and psychologically before, during, and after eating?

Yoga, tai chi, and qigong

Some types of exercise, such as the following, are especially effective at promoting relaxation. Try working some or all of these activities into your routine.

■ **Yoga.** Based on Indian philosophy, yoga is an excellent way to develop body awareness and elicit the relaxation response. The many different types of yoga share certain basic elements: pranayamas (rhythmic breathing), meditation, and asanas (stretching postures). Like tai chi and qigong, yoga increases flexibility and coordination, releases muscle tension, and enhances tranquility.

A study conducted at Ohio State University's Institute for Behavioral Medicine Research highlights the benefits of regular, sustained yoga practice. Although yoga delivered a mood boost both to yoga novices and experts, it seemed to help the experts—women who had practiced yoga once or twice weekly for at least two years—recover from stressful events more rapidly than novices did.

Researchers assessed certain physiological responses before and after the women participated in three activities: practicing yoga, walking slowly on a treadmill, and watching a video. The study also measured these responses before and after certain stress-inducing events. The researchers found that blood levels of the stress-related compound interleukin-6 (IL-6), which is suspected of playing a part in conditions such as type 2 diabetes and cardiovascular disease, were 41% higher in the yoga novices as compared with the yoga experts. The novices also experienced higher heart rates than the experts when they were exposed to various stress-inducing events.

Other studies have found additional benefits. One small study showed that yoga improved lung function in people with asthma, allowing them to use less medication to control the condition. In another study, regular yoga practice for at least four years contributed to an average weight loss of five pounds in overweight, middle-aged adults tracked for 10 years. Because yoga wasn't vigorous enough to account for that much additional calorie expenditure in these individuals, the researchers theorized that it might have affected weight by lowering concentrations of cortisol. Or, possibly, that the mindfulness cultivated by practicing yoga helped create a heightened awareness of the body—a state of mind that translated into healthier eating and exercise habits.

Yoga is an excellent way to elicit the relaxation response.

■ **Tai chi.** A series of slow, fluid, circular motions that originated as a martial art, tai chi especially benefits older people. By enhancing balance and muscle strength, it helps prevent falls that can lead to fractures—nearly halving the risk for falls in one study of older adults—and girds against gradual decline in physical function. Its low-intensity movements produce declines in blood pressure similar to those achieved with moderate-intensity aerobics, according to a randomized study of sedentary adults ages 60 or older.

Some doctors recommend tai chi for people with osteoarthritis as a way to reduce joint swelling and improve range of motion. And lower levels of reported stress, less pain, greater confidence in moving, and better balance were shown by people with rheumatoid arthritis ages 33 to 70 who practiced tai chi twice a week for 12 weeks.

■ **Qigong.** This ancient Chinese art melds breathing, meditation, gentle exercise, and flowing movements. Qi, or chi, is the Chinese word for the life energy believed to course through the body. Qigong aims to unblock and properly balance the flow of qi. When practiced regularly, it can lower your blood pressure, pulse, and demand for oxygen. These effects are all components of the relaxation response. Qigong may also enhance balance and flexibility.

Repetitive prayer

Around the world, faith traditions are as deeply rooted as they are varied. If these roots help you feel grounded, a short repetitive prayer could be a good way for you to elicit the relaxation response. When prayer is meaningful, the repetition of a such a prayer can enhance the relaxation response and possibly your health as well (see "The power of prayer and an active spiritual life," page 32).

To reap benefits from a repetitive prayer, it helps to believe that God is in your corner in this effort and has

The power of prayer and an active spiritual life

Several large studies suggest that people with an active religious life tend to stay healthier, live longer, and be happier. For example, a review article in the *Journal of the American Geriatrics Society* cited an international study of nearly 170,000 men and women from 14 countries that found religious affiliation and attendance at services significantly increased the likelihood of happiness and satisfaction. Twelve years of data from 2,800 older adults enrolled in the Yale Health and Aging Study, reported in *The Journals of Gerontology*, showed members of religious congregations had a slower onset of physical disability. Other studies on how religion affects health have noted less hostility and anxiety, lower blood pressure, and better quality of life among people with strong beliefs.

But the power of prayer is not easy to document. One study in *Annals of Behavioral Medicine* sifted through research claiming religion and spirituality have positive effects on cardiovascular disease and high blood pressure. The investigators disputed the results, citing numerous flawed or irrelevant supporting studies.

Still, prayer clearly offers solace and comfort to many people. Religious communities can be part of a larger social network that keeps a person afloat with emotional support and down-to-earth assistance. By reinforcing positive emotions, religious belief might stimulate healthy physiological responses through complex nervous system pathways, much as a constant flood of negative thoughts may set the opposite reaction in motion. And, of course, certain religions encourage healthy habits, such as avoiding alcohol and tobacco.

given your body an inborn ability to heal itself. Believing in the healing power of mind-body approaches—and specifically in the power of the prayer you've chosen to aid you—will help, too.

Keeping those points in mind, choose a favorite short prayer from your faith, or a phrase from it, to use as your focus when you elicit the relaxation response (see "Eliciting the relaxation response," page 24). Examples of prayers that can be deeply meaningful are

- The Lord is my shepherd
- Hail Mary, full of grace
- Sh'ma Yisrael
- Insh'Allah
- May all beings be filled with joy and peace
- Om.

Even if you do not belong to a particular religious faith—as is true of 16% of Americans, according to a recent Pew Forum survey—a meaningful secular prayer may have a place in your relaxation response repertoire. For example, you might consider choosing a phrase, such as "Grant me serenity," from a secular version of the Serenity Prayer.

Expanding your toolbox for managing stress

Although eliciting the relaxation response helps enormously in controlling stress, it works best when combined with other tools for stress management. Eating well, exercising, socializing, and cognitive restructuring are among the tools that can help you reduce stress and recharge your personal energy battery, topping it up, rather than draining it day by day, as the frequent arousal of the stress response does. This section also describes ways to reframe negative thoughts, communicate better, and learn life-enhancing lessons from positive psychology. Most likely, you'll find that a combination of approaches will work best for you. As with the relaxation response, we recommend sampling all of the options to decide which will prove most helpful.

Cognitive restructuring

Stop for a moment and try to remember the thoughts that were running through your head the last time you were late for work. Perhaps a simple thought, such as "the train is late," quickly transformed into "I'll be late to work. I won't make it to my meeting on time. My job is in jeopardy."

Sometimes even seemingly happy thoughts hurtle down the same track. "Wonderful, the lab report says my biopsy results are negative!" can quickly turn to "Is that lab reliable? Maybe I have cancer, but the lab didn't pick it up. Cancer that's undetected gets worse. By the time the error is found, it could be too late."

Scenarios like these are examples of negative automatic thinking, which can engage the stress response almost as easily as a growling Doberman bounding in your direction. Consider, too, the barrage of negative thoughts that many people play through their minds on an endless loop, or flip on automatically when faced with certain people or situations. Familiar examples include: "I look awful," "I can't do this," "I'm stupid," "I'm such a screw-up," and "I'm a loser."

Is your energy battery charged?

Energy is a renewable resource. Imagine that you have a personal energy battery that recharges or drains as your life unfolds. Too much stress can deplete it, if you're not taking steps to manage that stress. Do you take enough time to recharge your battery—or are you frequently running on empty? Look at our examples and then try this exercise on your own. The first time you try it, don't be surprised if the list on the left outweighs the one on the right.

– WITHDRAWALS (drains on your energy)	+ DEPOSITS (charges your battery)
Not enough sleep last night; feeling so-so, but had to get to work	Went to bed early several nights this week so I'm feeling rested
Argument with my teenager before I left home	Had a chance to do breathing exercises
Hectic workday	My boss complimented me on a job well done
Ate lunch in 10 minutes at my desk	Spent 15 minutes of my lunch hour walking
Plumbing problem at home	Caught up with a friend by phone and made a date for a movie this weekend
Squabbled with my spouse over calling a plumber	Did a mini-relaxation in the time it took my old computer to start up
Didn't make it outside for a walk—it was raining anyway!	Started a new novel I've been wanting to read
Got caught in bad traffic	Tried stress reduction while stuck in traffic
Rushed home after doing errands to make dinner	Ate a tasty dinner with fresh vegetables and herbs

Feeling charged? Congratulations! Keep recharging your energy battery regularly to counter stress.

Feeling drained? Try to work toward fewer withdrawals and more deposits. You'll be surprised at how much a few small changes can do for you. Flip to "Your portable guide to stress relief" (page 45) to choose simple stress-easing strategies.

Are you facing major stressors? Combining several stress-reducing tools and techniques—regularly evoking the relaxation response (see "Managing your stress through the relaxation response," page 24), applying better communication and cognitive restructuring skills (see "Cognitive restructuring," at left), and finding ways to nurture body and mind (see "Nurturing yourself," page 42)—will be most helpful.

The voice may be yours or that of someone else from your life, such as an overly critical parent. Even in the absence of obviously stressful situations, this inner critic can make you miserable and stressed. When this happens, picture yourself swatting gnats—that is, NATs, as some experts call these negative automatic thoughts—flying around your head.

Often, our negative thoughts are riddled with irrational distortions. But take heart. You needn't knuckle under to negative thoughts. A type of therapy called cognitive behavioral therapy is built on the premise that thoughts and perceptions shape moods and emotions—and that distorted thinking can be changed with practice. You can learn to deflate them through cognitive restructuring, a technique that helps you change the way you think. That, in turn, can help you change how you feel.

Recognizing your distortions

Ten common cognitive distortions appear below. They are based on theories of cognitive therapy expounded by Dr. Aaron T. Beck, which were further refined and brought to popular attention by Dr. David D. Burns. Do any of these distortions resonate with you? Use this list to help make you aware of ingrained negative thought patterns and try to substitute more realistic, positive thoughts.

- **All or nothing.** Everything is black or white; nothing is gray. If you don't perform flawlessly, you consider yourself a complete failure.
- **Overgeneralization.** One negative event—such as a slight from your spouse or partner or an encounter with a dishonest merchant—is perceived to be part of an endless pattern of dismaying circumstances and defeat. For example, you might think, "He's always cold" or "You can't trust anyone."
- **Mental filter.** One negative episode, such as a rude comment made to you during an otherwise enjoyable evening, shades everything like a drop of food coloring in a glass of water. It's as though you are filtering out all the light and only see darkness.
- **Disqualifying the positive.** You are unable or unwilling to accept a compliment or praise. You deflect all compliments with self-deprecation. You might say, "It's no big deal" or "It was nothing."
- **Jumping to conclusions.** You draw negative conclusions without checking to see if they have any foundation in fact. You may be mind-reading: "My friend seems upset; she must be mad at me." Or you may be fortune-telling: "I just know the results of my medical test won't be good."
- **Magnification or minimization.** You exaggerate potential problems or mistakes until they take on the proportions of a catastrophe. Or you minimize anything that might make you feel good, such as appreciation for a kind act you did or the recognition that other people have flaws, too.
- **Emotional reasoning.** You assume your negative emotions reflect the way things are. For example, "I feel inferior. Therefore, I must not be as good as others." Often these emotions are residual feelings that linger from other experiences in your past.
- **"Should" statements.** You adhere to a rigid set of beliefs and internal rules about what you "should" be doing and feel guilty when you don't stay the course.
- **Labeling.** Rather than describe a mistake or challenge in your life, you label yourself negatively: "I'm a screw-up." When another person's behavior bothers you, you pin a global label on him or her: "She's so controlling."
- **Personalization.** You blame yourself for triggering a negative event that occurred for complex reasons or for something that was largely out of your control: "If I had taken care of myself properly, I never would have gotten cancer."

Other clues can also help you identify distorted thinking. Sentences that include the words "must," "should," "ought," "always," and "never" are often harsher than necessary and reflect rigid thinking that could stand to be softened.

Stop, breathe, reflect, choose

If you're like most people, some of the distortions listed above sound awfully familiar. The next step is learning how to challenge these overly simplistic, negative thoughts that cause you unnecessary distress. It's easiest, of course, when the thoughts are patently untrue: "I never do anything right," for example. It's harder when there's an element of truth mixed in with simplistic falsehoods: "At my age, I know I'll

Massage: Putting stress relief in other hands

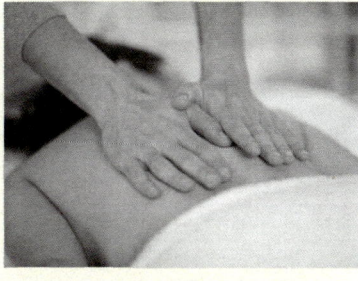

A massage at the hands of a skilled practitioner can be rejuvenating. Research shows massage has a physiological impact, too. Massage lowers blood pressure and heart rate and may enhance certain measures of immune function. Massage has been found to boost the activity of pleasure-related brain chemicals in people with a broad range of physical and psychological conditions. Some research suggests it lowers levels of the stress hormone cortisol, though not all studies agree on this.

One study showed that women with breast cancer who participated in massage therapy three times a week for five weeks experienced more immune system activity and reported less depression, anxiety, and fatigue than the women who didn't receive massages regularly. Some studies have found that massage is also beneficial in boosting the immune systems of people with HIV.

Whether it's for therapeutic reasons or purely for pleasure, massage offers the comforts of a warm touch and release from muscle tension. Experienced practitioners can be found through professional organizations, such as the American Massage Therapy Association (www.amtamassage.org or toll-free at 877-905-0577) and the National Certification Board for Therapeutic Massage and Bodywork (www.ncbtmb.org or toll-free at 800-296-0664).

---

never reach my goals." If you always longed to be a famous opera singer but lacked the time and talent to bring your dream to fruition, that statement may apply. For one goal. Most likely, though, you could list other goals that you did reach. And if you recast your dream by realizing that you enjoy singing, whether in the Metropolitan Opera or a community chorus, you could set course for a new goal and actually meet it.

This four-step process taught at the Benson-Henry Institute for Mind Body Medicine is one way to help derail stress that stems from distortions and negative thoughts:

■ **Stop.** Consciously call a mental time-out when you feel stressed. By saying "Stop," you can halt the negative stress cycle in its tracks.

■ **Breathe.** Take a few deep breaths to reduce physical tension and step back from the stressor before you react.

■ **Reflect.** Ask yourself the following questions: Is this thought or belief true? Did I jump to a conclusion? What evidence do I actually have? Is there another way that I could view the situation? What's the worst that could happen? Does it help me to think this way?

■ **Choose.** Decide how to deal with the source of your stress. For example:

- Problem solve what you can control. Gather information, ask advice, make a plan, and take action.
- Accept what you cannot change—a death, perhaps—drawing meaning from it, if possible. Have empathy for yourself; seek social support, as appropriate; express feelings and seek counseling if needed; use your stress management tools.
- Challenge distorted, irrational thinking and adjust your view of reality using cognitive restructuring techniques. Remember, many things we worry about never come to fruition. Ask yourself the following questions: How else can I think about this? What else can I do to cope more effectively?

Here's an example of how it might work. If you get stuck in traffic on the way to work, stop and notice stress signs such as a tight neck and shoulders. Try to relax and take a few deep breaths. Reflect: "It's just a traffic jam. I can handle this. It's not worth getting this upset." Don't assume you'll be fired. Tell yourself, "I'll just be a few minutes late. I'm doing the best I can. I can handle this."

Schedule your worries

You may find it helps to structure your worry—either by setting aside a time to worry or creating a place to "hold" your worries (see "Make a worry box," page 46). These techniques can help you keep negative thoughts and fears from weaving their way throughout your days.

Call a time-out for yourself if your mind is racing, you feel overwhelmed and anxious, and you can't seem to focus. Set a timer for 15 minutes and write down everything that you're worried about. But when the buzzer sounds, put your worries away and allow yourself to be fully present. Try to accept your concerns and fears without judgment. Practicing mindfulness meditation may help with this task (see "Mindfulness meditation," page 29).

If you are going through a tumultuous or difficult time—perhaps you are in the midst of a divorce or facing a financial setback—and worry is persistent, setting aside a specific time each day to record your worries may help.

Consider the goose in a bottle

When you find yourself jumping to conclusions or dwelling on negative thoughts, the "goose in the bottle" exercise may help challenge your thinking. The exercise has its roots in a well-known Zen koan that asks us to consider how to free a goose from a glass bottle. In this story, an official asks a Zen master to imagine this problem: a man places a gosling in a bottle, feeding it through the neck of the bottle until it is fully grown and there is no room in the bottle anymore. How can the man get the goose out without harming it or breaking the bottle? The master imagines the scene and then shouts, "See! The goose is out."

The mind created this problem; the goose was imagined in the bottle and can just as easily be imagined out of it. The story is a reminder that worry is the misuse of imagination.

The next time you are playing out worst-case scenarios or allowing negative thoughts to snowball, stop and picture the goose. Ask yourself: "Is this just a goose in a bottle?" And consider how else you can think about the situation.

A healthy plate

Nurturing your body by eating well helps build resiliency and lays a solid foundation for wellness. What you put on your plate has a big role in your risk of developing many illnesses, including high blood pressure, heart disease, diabetes, and cancer, which will certainly affect your overall stress level. Obesity due to overeating is linked with many ailments, too. It's also a source of emotional stress for millions of Americans who are continually reminded of their failure to achieve the slim look idolized in this culture.

But what should you eat? Questionable dietary advice and commercial agendas often drown out objective scientific recommendations on what to eat. That's why experts from the Harvard School of Public Health teamed up with Harvard Health Publications to come up with a visual approach to healthy eating based on data gathered from thousands of men and women enrolled in well-designed, long-term studies. Harvard's Healthy Eating Plate (see Figure 7, at left) clarifies and amplifies MyPlate from the U.S. Department of Agriculture, pointing you to the healthiest choices among the major food groups.

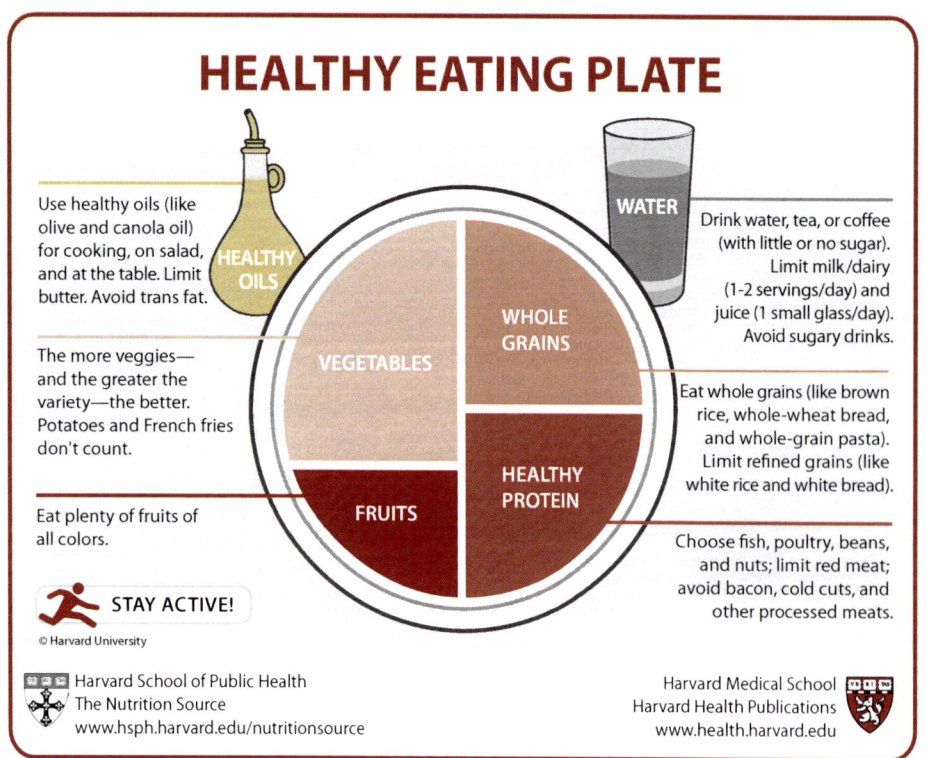

Figure 7: Harvard's Healthy Eating Plate

When you look at the Healthy Eating Plate, does it resemble what you normally eat? If so, wonderful—you're fueling your body with plenty of healthy foods. Many of us can't make that claim, though. Rather than chide yourself for less than stellar eating habits, consider a few simple changes to strengthen your current diet. Could you add a half-cup serving of vegetables and fruit to your daily fare—maybe slip it in as an afternoon snack? Could you expand your color palette, choosing a range of deep-hued vegetables and fruits, which tend to have more antioxidants and important nutrients? Could you try one new vegetable or fruit every week? Could you replace some unhealthy fats (such as those found in meat, cheese, and most commercial baked goods) with healthier sources (such as olive or canola oil and fats found in nuts and cold-water fish like salmon)? Could you choose whole grains like brown rice, barley, whole wheat, and quinoa more often than refined grains like white rice or white flour? These simple steps can have a real impact on your health.

Mindful eating

Food offers comfort and pleasure as well as nourishment. Gulping down fast food while changing lanes on the freeway, however, offers none of these benefits. We're a culture in a rush, which influences how we eat. Fast-food meals often replace family mealtimes, and the practice of eating while driving has become such a cultural phenomenon that the term "dashboard dining" has been coined to describe it. But the problem with eating fast and furiously is the likelihood of eating more than you intend—not to mention the less than healthy choices that are generally available on the run. Taking the time to eat mindfully can renew your enjoyment of food. It will also help you manage how much you eat, since it takes 20 minutes from the time you start eating for the "fullness signal" in the brain to kick in. Thus, when you rush through a meal, you may well eat more than necessary because you continue to eat until your brain registers that your body is satisfied.

Instead, try to take the time to savor each bite. To practice mindful eating, sidestep distractions like the background drone of TV or even a propped-up book. Start by setting a place for yourself and sitting

> **Tips for controlling how much you eat**
>
> ✔ Eat from smaller plates; large plates encourage taking bigger helpings.
>
> ✔ Start your meal with a hot beverage such as tea, soup, or broth. Hot drinks feel more filling than cold ones and can help you avoid overeating.
>
> ✔ Enjoy meals more by eating mindfully, one bite at a time. Savor sensations, paying attention to sight, scent, taste, and texture (see "Mindful eating," at left).
>
> ✔ If you're still hungry at the end of the meal, choose a piece of fruit instead of a second helping.
>
> ✔ Before snacking, take a deep breath and ask yourself if you really are hungry or whether anxiety, boredom, or loneliness is driving your desire to eat. Try drinking a glass of water to see if that fills you up. Practice satisfying stress or emotional hungers in new ways, perhaps by going for a walk or calling a friend.

down. Close your eyes for several seconds, and inhale and exhale deeply to help yourself focus. Bring your full attention to the moment. Now, look at your food. Breathe in its aromas before you taste it. Chew slowly so you can delight in textures and flavors. Try not to rush through one mouthful to get to the next, but concentrate instead on the mouthful you're actually eating at that moment. Bringing all your senses into play can sharpen your taste for fresher, healthier foods and help break the cycle of stress-related eating.

In addition, pay attention to how you feel before you begin to eat, while you're eating, and afterward. Are you feeling physical signs of hunger, or is it simply "time" for dinner? Are you eating to quell stress? As you become more aware of your feelings, you may find other stress control techniques just as satisfying as eating.

Physical activity

If exercise were available as a pill, experts say, everyone would be taking it. That's because accumulating 30 minutes a day of moderate-intensity activity—a brisk walk, for example, or even housework—delivers a wealth of health-enhancing benefits. Exercise improves cholesterol levels, lowers blood pressure, helps keep bones strong and healthy, and enhances the immune system. It can boost metabolism and mood.

What's more, exercise defuses stress. If you exercise shortly after the stress response is engaged—let's say by sprinting away from an oncoming bus—you burn off stress hormones just as nature intended. No bus handy? Just about any form of motion helps relieve pent-up muscle tension. And certain activities, such as yoga, tai chi, and qigong (see page 30), and rhythmic, repetitive exercise, such as walking, running, swimming, bicycling, and rowing, elicit the relaxation response, too. Regularly engaging in these kinds of activities can help you ward off everyday stress.

To boost the stress-relief rewards, you'll need to shift your attention to become aware of yourself—what and how you're feeling—and your surroundings during exercise. This should leave you feeling calmer and more centered. This approach works as well on nature walks as it does during as strength training. As you lift and plant each foot, or as you raise and lower the weights, coordinate your breathing with your movements, focusing your attention mindfully on the sensations in your body.

Once you get under way, become aware of how your breathing complements the activity. Breathe rhythmically, repeating the focus word, phrase, or prayer you've chosen. Remember to adopt a passive attitude. When disruptive thoughts intrude, gently turn your mind away from them and focus on moving and breathing.

A mindful walk

Taking a mindful walk is a good example of exercising with relaxation in mind. As you move and breathe rhythmically, be aware of the sensations of your body. How does it feel as your breath flows in through your nostrils and out through your mouth? Gradually expand your awareness to the sights and smells around you. Notice the freshly mown grass, flowers, trees, fallen leaves, dappled sun, or gray clouds. How does the outside air feel against your body? How does the surface beneath your feet feel and sound? What thoughts are moving through your head? A slow, mindful walk helps center and relax you. Alternatively, a brisker pace that pushes your limits can be calming and energizing in equal parts. In this case, place more emphasis on the sensations of your body, such as your quickened breathing and heartbeat and the way your muscles respond as you tax them.

Safety first

A few words of care are in order:
- If you aren't normally active, or if you have health problems or a painful or disabling condition, speak with your doctor before beginning any exercise program.
- When you exercise, listen to your body. Perform only movements that feel comfortable to you. As you grow stronger or more limber, you can gradually expand your range.
- Try to integrate deep, calm breathing into your routine. You may find it easiest to first familiarize yourself with the movements of the exercises you select and then combine them with deep breathing.
- If you wish to try yoga, tai chi, or qigong, join a class with an experienced instructor who can help you learn the movements correctly and adapt the program to your needs.

Better ways to communicate

Communicating effectively is a powerful tool. It helps ward off the stress you experience from behaving either too passively or too aggressively. Learning to listen actively and communicate assertively can improve your ability to manage conflicts, prevent situations from escalating, and lessen the likelihood of stressful misunderstandings.
- To listen actively, appreciate other people's realities without making judgments or interrupting. This kind of empathetic listening takes practice, but it can make a difference in the tone discussions take.
- To speak assertively, use calm, unemotional language that acknowledges the other person's perspective and allows your own opinion to be heard. By doing so, you relay the message that "I count and you count."

Try this exercise to practice listening actively and speaking assertively. First, find a partner. Start by taking the role of the communicator while your partner is the listener. As the communicator, tell your partner about a stressful or frustrating experience. Use clear, calm, assertive language. Avoid accusations such as "You always make me feel…" and stick to first-person language such as "I feel ____ when you ____." Meanwhile, the listener should listen and resist the urge to interrupt. Then, switch roles. At the end of the exercise, take turns paraphrasing what each of you heard your partner say and how you think they were feeling. Ask for validation. How did it feel to be listened to without interruption or judgment? Think about how you can use these techniques in real-life situations, especially those you find stressful or contentious.

Lessons from positive psychology

What helps us thrive as we move through life? Answers are starting to emerge from the field of positive psychology—a burgeoning field recognized by the American Psychological Association that studies factors that contribute to our well-being instead of searching for the roots of unhappiness. Researchers investigate the ingredients of a good life and weigh the effects of traits like optimism, humor, and even eccentricity. Many experts who design stress management programs now harness its principles.

Optimists, for example, tend to do better than pessimists when coping with stressful situations. They are more likely to put a positive spin on stressors, look for ways to make the best of a bad situation, and use problem-solving strategies to tackle difficulties.

Optimists may fare better physically, too. In a long-term study, adults classified as pessimists had a 19% higher risk of dying over the course of 30 years than did those identified as optimists. Other research suggests that a sense of optimism may offer some protection against heart disease. Some studies show it decreases levels of cortisol, which plays into high blood pressure, suppresses immune function, and lowers levels of certain inflammatory markers that may contribute to type 2 diabetes and atherosclerosis, the buildup of fatty deposits in arteries that can cause heart attacks and strokes.

If you're not a natural optimist, this information could merely fuel your pessimism. Don't let it. Take a deep breath and relax. Evidence suggests that avoiding

Boost your happiness and well-being

Looking for ways to feel happier and fight off depression? One study found that these exercises deliver positive results, particularly when they are done regularly.

- **Three good things in life.** For the next week, each night reflect on your day and find three things that went really well. Spend 10 minutes writing about them in a journal. It's important to write these down, rather than simply noting them in your head. These things could be as simple as reading a bedtime story to your toddler or having your spouse pick up ice cream for dessert. Then, next to each positive event, answer this question: "Why did this good thing happen?" For example, a wife might write that her husband picked up ice cream "because my husband is really thoughtful sometimes."

- **Using signature strengths in a new way.** The study participants were asked to fill out a character survey that identified their top five strengths. The survey is available online at www.authentichappiness.sas.upenn.edu. You can take the survey or alternatively, simply reflect on your own character and try to find five qualities that are your strong suits. You may want to ask a supportive friend or family member to help you identify these character strengths. After doing this, choose one of your strengths, and every day for the next week, try to use it in a different way.

- **A gratitude visit.** Identify someone who has been particularly kind to you whom you haven't thanked properly—perhaps a parent, friend, teacher, coach, teammate, or employer. In the next week, write a letter of gratitude to that person and then hand-deliver it. Make your letter as specific as possible, spelling out what the person did for you, how often you remember those efforts, and what effect they had on you. When you meet, read your letter aloud to the recipient. Afterward, think about the following questions: How did you feel as you wrote your letter? How did the other person react to your letter, and how were you affected by the reaction? Is there someone else you would like to express your gratitude to in a similar way?

Adapted from the work of Martin E.P. Seligman, Ph.D., director of the University of Pennsylvania Positive Psychology Center and author of Authentic Happiness (Free Press, 2002) and Flourish (Atria, 2013).

pessimism is more important than boosting optimism. While it's true that there are people with naturally sunny natures, it's equally true that the way you handle yourself emotionally owes a great deal to nurture. With practice, your current outlook and behaviors can change for the better.

Well-being encompasses far more than optimism or simple questions surrounding happiness. Martin Seligman, the director of the University of Pennsylvania Positive Psychology Center and a leader in the field, ticks off five elements that feed into well-being: positive emotions, including happiness and a sense of satisfaction; deep engagement in tasks and joys; bonds forged through relationships; meaning in life; and achievement. Like the five fingers on your hand, you can learn to exercise each element individually, yet the quintet is strongest when working together.

Quite possibly, you've already tried some techniques used in positive psychology. These include reframing negative thoughts and journal writing, as well as emphasizing the importance of intimate bonds (see "Social support," at right). Other techniques help people tap into a sense of gratitude and thankfulness or simply a sense of humor. All of these therapeutic approaches amplify the positive.

In one study, researchers assessed how effective several different "happiness exercises" were at increasing happiness and decreasing depressive symptoms. They began by asking 577 adults to perform one of five different happiness exercises or a control exercise for the sake of comparison (writing down their early memories every night for one week). The participants completed two surveys—a happiness index and a depression scale—before and after performing the exercises.

Two of these exercises—"Three good things in life" and "Using signature strengths in a new way"—had lasting effects, increasing happiness and decreasing depressive symptoms for as long as six months. The researchers had asked the participants to perform these exercises for one week, but in follow-up interviews they found that those who continued the exercises on their own got better, longer-lasting results. Another exercise, "Gratitude visit," delivered the best initial results—boosting happiness scores and lowering depressive symptoms considerably—but the effects disappeared by the three-month mark. (See "Boost your happiness and well-being," page 39, for information on how to perform all three exercises.)

In addition, there have been many intriguing studies on humor. Researchers have found that laughter boosts immune system activity and lowers the amount of circulating stress hormones, such as epinephrine and cortisol. No wonder many mind-body practitioners prescribe laughter. They often urge their patients to rent funny movies, read amusing books, and embrace the absurd in daily life.

Social support

Just as a boat is protected by the rubber bumpers that separate it from a hard dock, so, too, do people benefit

▶ Affirmations

Affirmations are statements that express love, acceptance, and, often, a joyous vision for your self and your life. A stream of positive thoughts can drown out more negative ones. Try incorporating simple affirmations, such as "I breathe in healing" or "I breathe out tension," into relaxation techniques. Or paste them to your mirror or another prominent place where you can read them several times a day. The more often you repeat an affirmation, the more likely you are to believe it and act on it.

Whether you write your own affirmation or borrow one from a helpful bumper sticker, the words should resonate for you. When creating an affirmation, choose a stressful aspect of your life and decide what a positive outcome would be or how you wish you felt about the situation. Try to craft statements in first person and present tense, such as these:

- "I can do this."
- "It's just a bump in the road."
- "I can handle this situation."
- "I am doing my best."
- "I am calm."
- "I deserve respect."
- "Week by week, I am growing healthier and stronger."
- "I can relax my body."
- "I am a loving, caring person."
- "I like myself."

when social buffers soften the inevitable bumps and bruises of life. Studies show that social ties—at least those that represent positive relationships—significantly protect health and well-being.

In Sweden, researchers following more than 17,000 men and women for six years found that the group that reported the most isolation and loneliness had almost four times the risk of an early death as those with good social networks. California researchers who tracked roughly 7,000 Alameda County residents for nine years found that a lack of strong community and social bonds multiplied the likelihood of dying during the study period by nearly two to three times.

Our confidants, friends, acquaintances, co-workers, relatives, and spouses or companions weave a life-enhancing social net. Their support may involve outright assistance or may be largely emotional. Studies show that people who have greater social support fare better on measures of immune function when faced with stressors as diverse as caregiving, surgery, exams, and job strain. For example, women with breast cancer who felt they had high-quality emotional support from an intimate relationship, social support from a doctor, and nourishment from other connections had more natural killer cells—capable of destroying virus-laden cells and certain tumor cells—than those who lacked these advantages.

Not surprisingly, the quality of relationships counts. Research suggests that negative ones—such as an embattled marriage or a draining caretaking arrangement—can be more harmful than helpful. One study of women with breast cancer who were living with a spouse or partner examined the effects of relationship stress on recovery. Researchers found that even five years after the original diagnosis, those in stressful relationships recovered more slowly—showing greater signs of psychological distress, poorer physical health, and a steeper reduction in physical activity—than their counterparts who were in stable relationships.

Strengthening your social bonds

Given the pleasures and benefits of social ties, why not grasp opportunities to expand your social circle and deepen the ties you've already made? Here are some ways to do just that:

- If you normally wait for others to reach out, pick up the phone and propose a date.
- Explore some of the many volunteer opportunities available, from wielding tools to help spruce up affordable housing to mentoring a child or businessperson. To find opportunities that fit your talents and interests, check with the organizations VolunteerMatch (www.volunteermatch.org) or Senior Corps (www.seniorcorps.org), or call your local chapter of the United Way.
- Embrace technology. Email, texting, tweeting, and, yes, even old-school telephones extend your reach around the world. Social media sites like Facebook, MySpace, and LinkedIn can help you connect with old friends or find new work opportunities. Libraries and senior centers offer free online time and possibly tech tips, or you can work on extending your e-reach by checking helpful how-to videos (try YouTube) or taking short classes.
- Find like-minded people through intriguing classes and organizations, or by harnessing social media engines that can link you to just about anyone interested in doing just about anything.
- Religion offers enormous support to many people around the world. If that's true for you, join in on services that suit your faith. If it's hard to get to religious services, ask fellow congregants to escort you. If a significant illness keeps you away, find out if your spiritual leader makes home visits.
- Remember that social support is a two-way street. Offer assistance to friends, family, and neighbors. Accept help or a hand reached out in friendship when it's offered to you.
- Share a confidence. Doing so can turn a friendly relationship into an even deeper one.
- Consider adopting a pet. Research shows that pets can have beneficial effects on your physical and emotional health. Plus, taking a dog for walks encourages you to be active and links you with like-minded animal lovers.
- If depression, low self-esteem, or social phobias affect your ability to make connections, seek help. Start by talking with your doctor. Many people have been aided by therapy, medications, or both.

Nurturing yourself

Learning to nurture yourself is another key tool for managing stress. While you may know a great deal about nurturing others, satisfying your own needs may not be second nature.

It's common wisdom, for example, that women put a larger percentage of their waking hours into nurturing others than men do. Whether or not women work outside the home, studies suggest that they spend more time than men do tending house and loved ones. If you're a woman, odds are good that you provide the emotional glue that holds relationships and families together. You buy the birthday cards and pick up the phone to offer help when someone is sick. When elderly parents, children, grandchildren, and spouses or partners need assistance, you do much of the work or coordinate necessary services. Our culture expects you to be self-sacrificing. Your needs may take last place; putting yourself first is cast as selfishness.

For men, our society places great emphasis on getting ahead. That can encourage a single-minded focus on career to the detriment of other activities. In this way, men are discouraged from indulging their nurturing side, although plenty of men flout these cultural stereotypes, especially after becoming fathers.

Just as women are pressed from the get-go to give to others, men tend to be pushed toward the receiving end. That creates imbalances and potential sources of distress for both sexes. If you're a woman, you may not feel comfortable taking time to refresh yourself. If you're a man, you may not have much practice creating your own nurturing rituals and, like your female counterpart, you may feel uneasy doing so. Clearly, both women and men can benefit from learning to focus on themselves in healthy, rejuvenating ways.

Learning to care for yourself

The art of nurturing yourself is not a single technique. Rather, it's an overarching concept for your life, says Harvard psychologist Alice D. Domar in her book *Self-Nurture*. The spark you gain from nurturing your imagination, career, relationships, sex life, or spiritual side amplifies the healing effects of other stress-relief techniques. The many, varied options for self-nurture include

- journal writing
- cognitive restructuring
- relaxation exercises
- affirmations and prayer
- social support
- creative, productive, and leisure activities.

Imagine these techniques and self-nurturing acts as dry seeds for a garden. Lush growth rewards those who do more than scratch the earth, toss in a few seeds, and step back to see what comes up. Dig deep. Water frequently. Remove choking weeds from the plot when necessary. Combining the richness of your past experiences, a willingness to expand your current boundaries, and a desire to fill your life with courage, love, and joy can make a great deal of difference in what you reap.

Creativity, productivity, and leisure

The nerve-jangling pressure of lengthy daily "to do" lists can leach away energy. The thought of adding more items to the list may fill you with more dismay than delight, even if the addition is relaxation, creativity, or time with a loved one. Yet when you refresh yourself in meaningful ways, you add to your stock of energy and joy.

What does "creativity" mean to you? Writing a short story? Sculpting clay? Designing a retreat? Pulling out a paint box? Dancing around the room? Building a deck? Cooking up a feast? Landscaping a garden?

If you have a dream you've never explored, find small and big ways to follow through. Sing in the shower, take lessons from a pro, or hit karaoke night to try out some tunes. You needn't audition for "The Voice" unless that's your dream.

If you have no idea where to turn, take a look online or sign up for a class you think you might enjoy. Give yourself the opportunity to try a variety of options. Don't give up if the first one fails to captivate you or if the results of your effort don't meet your expectations. Discover what creative work you love, and do it.

Productive work forges links between you and the world and invests life with meaning. It matters little whether tasks are performed via a paid or volunteer job or while digging in the garden. They offer pleasure and sometimes the chance to be creative.

If you're retired or find that the work that pays your bills offers few opportunities for satisfaction, indulge your productive side elsewhere. The simplest task, such as slicing vegetables for dinner or scrubbing a floor, may be less tedious and more joyful if you approach it mindfully. Jobs that involve other people can spark connections that nurture you in other ways. Work that helps others often offers special satisfactions. Such volunteer opportunities abound for people of every age and level of ability. Check online or call local volunteer organizations for tasks that fit your talents and available time.

The job many of us find hardest is setting aside time for pursuits defined as leisure. Reading a novel, playing a game of tennis, soaking in a hot bath, or spending a half-hour meditating may seem selfish when a lengthy "to do" list beckons. Productive and even creative pursuits are more likely to meet with accepting nods. Yet playfulness invites joy back into your life. And embracing such opportunities for relaxation enhances "flow," a state described by psychologist Mihaly Csikszentmihalyi in which creative juices are freed and their full expression is directed to all pursuits.

So, stretch out on a hammock for a nap. Enjoy a massage. Carve out 10 to 20 minutes during your busy day for breath focus or a body scan. Soak in the sounds of music you find calming or invigorating or simply pleasurable. Taking this time for yourself helps ward off exhaustion and burnout, allowing you to focus more attentively and less resentfully on the tasks of your day. Consider it a gift to yourself that ultimately pays dividends to others.

Journals: Managing stress the write way

If you're like most people, you've learned to bottle up "unacceptable" emotions, such as anger, fear, frustration, and grief. Sometimes, of course, the cap slips off. Then these emotions spill forth at high intensity, although not necessarily in the right direction. One safe way to decant any emotions—even the most hurtful, terrifying, or sad feelings—is journal writing. A blank sheet of paper and a pen, or a blank page on your computer, can offer enormous release and, possibly, insight into hidden conflicts.

Writing about traumatic events can have physical benefits, too, according to James W. Pennebaker, chair of psychology at the University of Texas at Austin, who worked on a series of classic studies requiring one group of people to write down their deepest thoughts and feelings about the most traumatic event they recalled. A control group wrote only about trivial events. Both groups wrote for 15 minutes a day for four days. In one study, the group that expressed deep emotions reported feeling better and also had significantly fewer doctors' visits and symptoms of illness for nearly half a year afterward. After a similar experiment, the group that revealed deep emotions had livelier immune system defenders called T cells for the next six weeks.

Journal writing can help relieve ongoing sources of stress.

Why does writing about emotional issues make a difference in physical and emotional health? Pennebaker theorizes that confiding bottled-up feelings relieves stress that otherwise would ratchet up blood pressure, heart rate, and muscle tension.

Writing it out

Clinicians at the Benson Henry Institute for Mind Body Medicine have found that the following journal exercise helps relieve ongoing sources of stress. A single attempt is not enough, though. When you first sit down to write about a problem, you may feel more anxious. The wound, once exposed, may initially hurt more than it did while hidden. But continuing to write about the same problem over the course of several days often enables you to work through difficult emotions and reach resolution or acceptance.

Here's some advice before you begin:
- Deeply troubling events and situations—such as domestic violence, rape, or direct exposure to acts of terrorism or war—are best explored with an experienced therapist. For other situations, you can proceed on your own and seek professional help only if you feel you need assistance.
- If you're physically healthy, choose the most stressful event or problem you currently face. It's usually one that you frequently dwell upon. Or, if you think your current problems stem from past circumstance, write about upsetting events in your past.
- Truly let go. Write down what you feel and why you feel that way.
- Write for yourself, not others. Don't worry about grammar or sentence structure. If you run out of things to say in the time allotted, feel free to repeat yourself.
- Do this exercise for 15 to 20 minutes a day for three to four days, or as long as a week if you feel writing continues to be helpful.

Bringing more joy to your life

You needn't only write about sources of stress. Another approach is to write about a positive event to identify ways to bring more joy and meaning to your life. For this exercise, set aside 10 minutes to write about any positive event that's taken place in your life. Perhaps it was having a baby, getting a coveted job, touring the French countryside, or getting an advanced degree. Focus on the details of the event as well as how you felt at the time. After you're done writing, take a few minutes to think about your feelings. Were you proud of a hard-won accomplishment? Exhilarated by a new experience? Awash in love and acceptance because of a connection with a loved one? Now look for ways to experience those feelings again. Can you find opportunities in the present that might bring you those same feelings?

SPECIAL SECTION

Your portable guide to stress relief

Pressed for time? Join the club. Whether you have one minute or half an hour, dipping into the seven stress-busting suggestions here will ease your day.

1 Take the sting out of 10 common stressors

Sometimes just thinking about embarking on a program of stress control can be stressful. Rather than freeze in your tracks, start small and bask in the glow of your successes. Give yourself a week to focus on practical solutions that could help you cope with just one stumbling block or source of stress in your life. Pick a problem described here and see if these suggestions work for you.

Frequently late? Apply time management principles. Consider your priorities (be sure to include time for yourself), then delegate or discard unnecessary tasks. Map out your day, segment by segment, setting aside time for different tasks, such as answering emails, writing memos, or returning phone calls. If you get caught up online, put away distractions—no texts, tweets, emails, or games—while you dive into tasks. If you are overly optimistic about travel time, consistently give yourself an extra 15 minutes or more to get to your destinations. If lateness stems from dragging your heels, consider the underlying issue. Are you anxious about what will happen after you get to work or to a social event, for example? Or maybe you're trying to jam too many tasks into too little time. Tracking time for various tasks can help you become more realistic.

Often angry or irritated? Consider the weight of cognitive distortions. Are you magnifying a problem, leaping to conclusions, or applying emotional reasoning? Take the time to stop, breathe, reflect, and choose (see page 34).

Unsure of your ability to do something? Don't try to go it alone. If the problem is work, talk to a coworker or supportive boss. Ask a knowledgeable friend, check reliable online sources, or call the local library or an organization that can supply the information you need. Write down other ways that you might get the answers or skills you need. Turn to CDs, books, or classes, for example, if you need a little tutoring. This works equally well when you're learning relaxation response techniques, too.

Overextended? Clear the deck of at least one time-consuming household task. Hire a housecleaning service, shop for groceries online, convene a family meeting to consider who can take on certain jobs, or barter with or pay teens—your own or local hires—for house or yard work. Consider what is truly essential and important to you and what might take a backseat right now.

Not enough time for stress relief? Try mini-relaxations (see page 47). Slow down to pay attention to every sensory aspect of a single task or pleasure. Or commit to one week of rising a bit early or paring down your schedule sufficiently to allow time to evoke the relaxation response every day.

www.health.harvard.edu

Stress Management

Feeling unbearably tense? Try massage, a hot bath, mini-relaxations, a body scan, or a mindful walk. Practically any exercise—a brisk walk, a quick run, a sprint up and down the stairs—will help, too. When done regularly, exercise wards off tension, just as relaxation response techniques do.

Frequently feel pessimistic? Remind yourself of the value of learned optimism: a more joyful life and, quite possibly, better health. Practice deflating cognitive distortions. Rent funny movies and read amusing books. Create a mental list of reasons you have to feel grateful. If the list seems too short, consider beefing up your social network and adding creative, productive, and leisure pursuits to your life.

Upset by conflicts with others? State your needs or distress directly, avoiding "you always" or "you never" zingers. Say, "I feel _____ when you _____." "I would really appreciate it if you could _____." "I need some help setting priorities. What needs to be done first and what should I tackle later?" If conflicts are a significant source of distress for you, consider a class on assertiveness training.

Worn out or burned out? Nurture yourself. Carve out time to practice relaxation response techniques or at least indulge in mini-relaxations. Care for your body by eating good, healthy food and for your heart by seeking out others. Give thought to creative, productive, and leisure activities. Consider your priorities in life: is it worth feeling this way, or is another path open to you? If you want help, consider what kind would be best. Do you want a particular task at work to be taken off your hands? Do you want to do it at a later date? Do you need someone with particular expertise to assist you?

Feeling lonely? Connect with others. Even little connections—a brief conversation in line at the grocery store, an exchange about local goings-on with a neighbor, a question for a colleague—can help melt the ice within you. It may embolden you, too, to seek more opportunities to connect. Be a volunteer. Attend religious or community functions. Suggest coffee with an acquaintance. Call a friend or relative you miss. Take an interesting class.

If a social phobia, low self-esteem, or depression is dampening your desire to reach out, seek help. The world is a kinder, more wondrous place when you share its pleasures and burdens.

---

2 Make a worry box

Everyone gets distracted by worries and concerns, but sometimes these worries can spill over, seeping into the fabric of your day. Having a place to contain your worries—quite literally—may help you set them aside so that you can focus on the more pleasurable or meaningful parts of your life.

Begin by finding or making a worry box. Any box will do. This is a great exercise for children, who may find it even more appealing if they can decorate the box as they like and keep it in a special place.

At the end of the day, take a few minutes to write down two or three of your concerns on slips of paper and place them inside the box. Or if the box is handy, you can write down worries as each crops up and drop your worries into the box throughout the day.

The worry box allows you to mentally let go of your worries. Once your worries are deposited in the box, try to turn your attention to other matters.

What you do with your slips of paper is up to you. Some people choose to throw out the notes without reading them again, while others benefit from looking through them periodically before tossing them away. In that case, you may be surprised to find that most of your worrying was fruitless, and that the scenarios you imagined never came to pass.

Your portable guide to stress relief | **SPECIAL SECTION**

3 Try a mini-relaxation

Mini-relaxations can help calm fear and reduce pain while you sit in the dentist's chair. They're equally helpful in thwarting stress before an important meeting, while stuck in traffic, or when faced with people or situations that annoy you. Here are a few quick mini-relaxation techniques to try.

Minis are intended to take only a few seconds to a few minutes, though you can do them for any amount of time you want. We recommend doing three to four mini-relaxation exercises daily.

Mini breath focus

Place your hand just beneath your navel so you can feel the gentle rise and fall of your belly as you breathe. Breathe in slowly. Pause for a count of three. Breathe out. Pause for a count of three. Continue to take a few slow, deep breaths.

Or alternatively, while sitting comfortably, take a few slow deep breaths and silently repeat to yourself "I am" as you breathe in and "at peace" as you breathe out. Repeat slowly two or three times. Then feel your entire body relax into the support of the chair.

Mini counting

Count down slowly from 10 to zero. With each number, take one complete breath, inhaling and exhaling. For example, breathe in deeply, saying "10" to yourself. Breathe out slowly. On your next breath, say "nine," and so on. If you feel lightheaded, count down more slowly to space your breaths further apart. When you reach zero, you should feel more relaxed. If not, go through the exercise again.

Mini body scan

While sitting down, take a break from whatever you're doing and check your body for tension. Relax your facial muscles and allow your jaw to fall open slightly. Let your shoulders drop. Let your arms fall to your sides. Allow your hands to loosen so that there are spaces between your fingers. Uncross your legs or ankles. Feel your thighs sink into your chair, letting your legs fall comfortably apart. Feel your shins and calves become heavier and your feet grow roots into the floor. Now breathe in slowly and breathe out slowly for a short while.

Mini massage

A combination of strokes you can do yourself works well to relieve muscle tension. Try gentle chops with the edge of your hands or tapping with fingers or cupped palms. Put fingertip pressure on muscle knots. Knead across muscles, and try long, light, gliding strokes. You can apply these strokes to any part of the body that falls easily within your reach.

For a short session like this, try focusing on your neck and head. Start by kneading the muscles at the back of your neck and shoulders. Make a loose fist and drum swiftly up and down the sides and back of your neck. Next, use your thumbs to work tiny circles around the base of your skull. Slowly massage the rest of your scalp with your fingertips. Then tap your fingers against your scalp, moving from the front to the back and then over the sides.

Now massage your face. Make a series of tiny circles with your thumbs or fingertips. Pay particular attention to your temples, forehead, and jaw muscles. Use your middle fingers to massage the bridge of your nose and work outward over your eyebrows to your temples.

Finally, close your eyes. Cup your hands loosely over your face and inhale and exhale easily for a short while.

Mini guided imagery

Start by sitting comfortably in a quiet room. Bring your awareness to your breath for a few minutes. Now picture yourself in a place that conjures up good memories. What do you smell—the heavy scent of roses on a hot day, crisp fall air, the wholesome smell of baking bread? What do you hear? Drink in the colors and shapes that surround you. Focus on sensory pleasures: the swoosh of a gentle wind; soft, cool grass tickling your feet; the salty smell and rhythmic beat of the ocean.

SPECIAL SECTION | Your portable guide to stress relief

4 Use mindfulness to reduce workday stress

Given an uncertain economy prompting job instability and the 24/7 pace technology has enabled us to achieve on the job, it is not surprising that 70% of Americans cite work as a significant source of stress in their lives, according to the most recent national survey from the American Psychological Association. Try these tips to take the edge off the stress you feel during your workday.

- While on the way to work, take a bit of time to do a body scan. If you're driving, loosen your death grip on the steering wheel, lower your tensed shoulders, and let your tight tummy relax.

- Stay in the right lane if driving and travel just at the speed limit. After you park, stay in your car for a minute and orient yourself to your day before going in to work.

- Take a five-minute break every few hours, but use this time to take a walk instead of simply pausing.

- Throughout your workday, monitor your tension levels and stress warning signs. Consciously try to relax and let go of your tension.

- Deliberately set aside a few minutes every hour or two to take some deep, diaphragmatic breaths.

- Have a mindful lunch in a new location, eating slowly and enjoying your time with yourself.

- At the end of your workday, think back on the day and acknowledge and congratulate yourself on your accomplishments.

- As you are driving home, be conscious of whether or not you are rushing. How does it feel? Try to slow down and relax.

- When you arrive home, change out of your work clothes, take some deep breaths to center yourself and, when possible, allow yourself five minutes of quiet before delving into activities there.

5 Harness the power of your mind

If you are feeling stressed or experiencing pain, these visualization exercises may help. They are especially effective once you have elicited the relaxation response because your brain is calmer and more focused, and you tend to be more open to suggestion and new information. Try making a recording of these visualizations—in either your own voice or that of a friend whose voice you find soothing.

Up, up, and away:
Hot-air balloon visualization

Imagine that you are standing beside a grassy meadow. Now, allow all of your senses to be present. Pay attention to every detail. Is it chilly outside? Can you see your breath? Or is it a warmer time of year? Is it sunny or cloudy? Continue to use all of your senses as you enter the meadow. What sounds do you hear? The wind? The rustle of leaves underfoot? Or the songs of birds or insects? Does the air smell of flowers? Or of dampness or leaves?

In the middle of the meadow is a colorful balloon. Come closer to it. Look carefully at the pattern of colors. You can choose to stay in the meadow and rest, or take a ride in the hot-air balloon.

If you choose to take a ride, slowly step into the basket. You see two small sandbags on the floor; on each sandbag are written words. Bend over and pick up one of the bags. This bag represents a burden, concern, or stress in your life. Notice what the words say, and then gently toss this bag over the side of the balloon basket. As you let go of the sandbag, the balloon gets lighter and lifts off the ground. Pick up the other sandbag. Notice what this bag represents. Toss this bag over the side and then sit comfortably down in the basket.

The balloon gets lighter and rises higher in the sky. You notice that with each burden you release, you also feel lighter and lighter just like the balloon. As you feel lighter, you begin to relax. Your muscles relax, and your mind becomes quiet. You might drift quietly among the clouds, floating lightly, feeling content, peaceful, and free of worries. Perhaps you choose to travel to a special or safe place. Sit quietly for several minutes, and continue to savor this time of silence with yourself.

It is time to begin your journey home. Remember that the balloon does not need the sandbags in order to land; there is no need to collect your burdens. Just leave them where they dropped. As the balloon slowly glides back toward the meadow, remember how it felt to release your burdens and concerns.

Focusing on how you felt during the balloon ride will help you repeat the experience when you feel stressed again in your daily life. Gently step out of the balloon and walk slowly back through the meadow, paying attention to your surroundings and being mindful of the experience of the moment. As you reach the edge of the meadow, transition back into the room, and become aware of the sights, sounds, and smells around you.

Evaporating pain: Visualization for headache sufferers

Close your eyes and try to imagine what your headache looks or feels like. Imagine that it is a hard steel band weighing down your forehead, eyelids, and nose. It is so hard that it is difficult for you to move the muscles in your face.

Now, you notice a dim, blue light appear. It settles above the hard steel band of headache and locks onto it. As the blue rays target your headache, the hard surface begins to soften. Gradually, it becomes softer and more pliable. You notice movement in the band like ripples on a lake. Take a few slow breaths, allowing the muscles of your face to relax.

The light continues to melt your pain. You feel your forehead loosen slightly as the hard band releases its grip. Now, the entire band is liquid, and it begins to evaporate. Your eyelids and forehead feel lighter as the liquid turns to steam, rising above your head. Your entire face relaxes as you see the last of the liquid disappear above you. You are engulfed in a soothing vapor. Your head and face feel light and relaxed, and you can breathe easily.

Now, focus on your breath. Take a few more slow, diaphragmatic breaths, paying attention to how peaceful and relaxed you feel. When you are ready, slowly open your eyes, stretch, and resume your day.

---

6 Keep a gratitude journal

Reflecting on the positive experiences, feelings, and relationships in your life can bring you greater joy. A gratitude journal is a good way to acknowledge what brightens your life and to help you turn your focus away from negative thoughts and feelings. It will also help you realize how many things in your life are actually going right.

Keep a journal by your bed so that at the end of each day, you can spend five to 10 minutes writing about something that you were grateful for in your day. Be as specific as possible. Don't just say "I love my family," but focus instead on concrete sights, sounds, and experiences, such as a hug from your child, a compliment from your partner, call from a friend, a sunset, or birds chirping outside your window. Celebrate accomplishments large and small—learning to master a new hobby, doing well on a project at work, or just getting the kids off to school on time.

Conjure up the scene in your mind and try to write about it in detail. Then, spend a few minutes soaking in the experience again. You can also use this journal to reflect on things from the past that you are grateful for.

7. Develop your personal plan for stress relief

Having a personalized stress-relief plan can help you manage stress when it strikes—or even keep it from building in the first place. Choose a variety of approaches, so that you can find the ones that work best for you. Remember, the more you practice, the easier the process gets.

Let the first column of Table 2, page 51, refresh your memory of your tools to help disarm the stress response. Then decide what you're willing to try and when you can do it. Even small changes—penciling in a few mini-relaxations to break up daily tasks, reconnecting with a friend over lunch, eating a healthy lunch, or taking a mindful walk—are important steps toward your goal. By writing down what you noticed after taking these steps, you can encourage yourself to keep at it. Try your plan for one or two weeks before you make any changes.

What if you don't stick to the schedule you've drawn up? Try not to feel discouraged. Consider what got in the way and whether you set out to do too much. Ask yourself what strategies could help you circumvent these obstacles next week. Finally, embrace what felt good and find the opportunity to repeat it. Practicing these techniques regularly should put you on the path toward a more peaceful, joyous, and healthy life.

Your portable guide to stress relief | **SPECIAL SECTION**

Table 2: My plan for stress management

WAYS TO HANDLE STRESS	THIS WEEK I WILL TRY	DAYS AND TIMES SET ASIDE	WHAT I NOTICED
Evoke the relaxation response through techniques such as breathing and a body scan (see "Managing your stress through the relaxation response," page 24).			
Identify your stress warning signs (see "My stress warning signs," page 22) and your negative thinking patterns (see "Cognitive restructuring," page 33).			
Practice communicating assertively and listening actively to reduce the chance of misunderstandings and frustration (see "Better ways to communicate," page 38).			
Nurture yourself by setting aside time for relaxation, eating well, exercising, connecting with others, and pursuing activities that add joy to your life (see "Nurturing yourself," page 42).			

www.health.harvard.edu   Stress Management

Resources

Organizations

Benson-Henry Institute for Mind Body Medicine at Massachusetts General Hospital
151 Merrimac St., 4th Floor
Boston, MA 02114
617-643-6090

and

Massachusetts General Hospital West
40 Second Ave., Suite 510
Waltham, MA 02451
781-487-6100
www.massgeneral.org/bhi

Home base to Dr. Herbert Benson and Aggie Casey (the medical editors of this report) and their colleagues, who have investigated the stress response and taught the relaxation response and other stress management approaches for many years, the institute offers programs for people with stress-related medical conditions, such as high blood pressure, chronic pain, cancer, or infertility. It also offers programs for exercise, nutrition counseling, yoga, wellness, and comprehensive stress management, as well as school-based programs for children and young adults.

Center for Mindfulness in Medicine, Health Care, and Society
55 Lake Ave. N.
Worcester, MA 01655
508-856-2656
www.umassmed.edu/cfm

Founded by Jon Kabat-Zinn, author of *Full Catastrophe Living*, the center offers information and programs on stress reduction. Its clinical treatment program is affiliated with the University of Massachusetts Medical School.

National Center for Complementary and Alternative Medicine (NCCAM)
9000 Rockville Pike
Bethesda, MD 20892
888-644-6226 (toll-free)
866-464-3615 (TTY)
www.nccam.nih.gov

Part of the National Institutes of Health, this government agency has a blog and a wealth of online publications on complementary and alternative medicine (CAM), as well as information specialists available by phone. It also conducts and supports valuable research on CAM.

Books

Grab a Tiger by the Toe: Stress-Proof Your Child
Marilyn Wilcher with Rana Chudnofsky and Laura Malloy
(Inkslingers Press ebook, 2012)

Written for parents of preschool through high school children, this book delves into common stresses that arise within families and explains the ways in which stress affects children at different ages. It contains a wealth of approaches for managing stress based on programs developed by the Benson-Henry Institute for Mind Body Medicine and tailored specifically for children.

Harvard Medical School Guide to Lowering Your Blood Pressure
Aggie Casey, M.S., R.N., and Herbert Benson, M.D.
(McGraw-Hill, 2005)

In this book, the medical editors of this report present an innovative, proven plan to lower your blood pressure. In addition to offering nutrition and exercise advice, the book describes a broad array of techniques that can help you manage your stress levels.

Managing Stress: Overcoming Stress in the Modern World
Joseph Shrand, M.D., with Leigh Devine, M.S.
(St. Martin's Griffin, 2012)

This self-care guide from Harvard Medical School knits together personal stories with explanations of what stress is and how it harms the body, then turns to a variety of techniques—including the relaxation response—to help manage it. Helpful chapters on handling severe stress and reducing the stress of people around you are included.

Mind Your Heart: A Mind/Body Approach to Stress Management, Exercise, and Nutrition for Heart Health
Aggie Casey, M.S., R.N., and Herbert Benson, M.D., with Ann MacDonald
(Free Press, 2004)

The medical editors of this report offer a balanced and holistic approach to heart health that combines lifestyle changes with cutting-edge medical procedures. The book discusses the importance of risk factors such as depression, anger and hostility, decreased social support, physical inactivity, and poor nutrition, and outlines self-care strategies to combat these problems.

Relaxation Revolution: Enhancing Your Personal Health Through the Science and Genetics of Mind Body Healing
Herbert Benson, M.D., and William Proctor
(Scribner, 2010)

The authors, including one of the medical editors of this report, present the latest scientific findings on how the mind can influence the body, including gene function. The book explores how people can harness the power of the mind to prevent life-threatening medical conditions, self-heal diseases, and supplement drugs and surgery—an approach that effectively constitutes the "third pillar" of medicine.

Say Goodbye to Stress
Jeff Brown, M.D., with Liz Neporent
(CSS Health, 2012)

A "Chicken Soup for the Soul" title that combines personal, often inspirational stories of people struggling with stressful situations in their lives with practical, step-by-step stress management tips.